Marie-José Van Hee architecten
More Home, More Garden

Marie-José Van Hee architecten
More Home, More Garden

This second, revised edition shares more home and more garden; over the last five years, new projects were finished and documented. We started to archive the extensive drawing collection, from which we made a selection for this book. Finally, you will find an updated project list highlighting work from 1977 until 2025, as well as the prizes awarded to Marie-José Van Hee.

Marie-José Van Hee architecten
More Home, More Garden

Quart Verlag
2025

Introduction

Katrien Vandermarliere

Praxis is the process by which a theory, lesson, or skill is enacted, practised, embodied or realised. It may also refer to the act of engaging, applying, exercising, realising or practising ideas.[1]

The oeuvre of Marie-José Van Hee has developed since the mid 1980s in Brussels and Flanders. During that era, building culture in Flanders became emancipated as a result of private engagement and support from cultural organisations. SAM (*Stichting Architectuurmuseum* / Architecture Museum Foundation) and the deSingel arts centre showed her emergent work at an early stage. After gaining practical experience through collaborations with Groep Planning, landscape architect Paul Deroose and architect Johan Van Dessel, amongst others, Van Hee established her own architectural practice. Over a period of almost 30 years, designing together with Paul Robbrecht and sharing a common office with Robbrecht en Daem architecten has become a constant activity that continues to this day.

Van Hee's architecture originates in architectural history, not so much in its theoretical or autonomous discourse, as in the way historical buildings are classified according to typologies and ensembles: urban dwellings and city walls, village squares and staircases, country lanes with barns and the iconic silhouette of a single tree. By referring to the culture of building, numerous classical architectural elements shape and define space: the galleries, the colonnades, the staircases with landings and the sequential positioning of windows and doors. The awareness of the built world and its relationship with the garden – and its extension, the landscape – cannot be left out. This preference for the intuitive and experiential is moulded in an understated and modest architecture, rooted in an immense respect for the logic of construction and the awareness of historically transferred knowledge, still present in the act of building today.[2]

Marie-José Van Hee is an architect with a vision who 'sees' places, spaces and proportions. She recognises, rearranges, redraws and creates something new from common knowledge. The initial design is formed by a basic concept that is quickly established, followed by a long process of thinking and drawing, negotiations between the client and her own experience, intuition and knowledge. Each time it yields a very precise project in which everything is extremely well thought out, consistent and correct. The result is a quiet architecture that does not strike a pose, yet evokes calmness and asceticism. The taut plan, the spatial arrangement, the purity of construction, all are intended to offer the freedom that architecture must give. Her buildings arrange space for living, in which personal, multiple use and versatility are key notions. Dwellings, communal housing, public buildings, bridge designs, the creation of public space … a diverse range of commissions in which the context – garden, landscape or city and urbanity – is always embraced by the designer.

This book is not a typical monograph with a chronological overview of projects; it is idiosyncratic in this respect. Instead, multiple points of view on the work of Marie-José Van Hee offer a compendium of meanings, insights and perceptions of her architecture. To approach this diversity in a fitting way, we chose an unusual but strict framework for this publication: three essays and an interview form the basic central content. A second structure organises the selection of eight buildings, each split into two groups of four projects. The private house of Van Hee is accentuated in the middle of the book. A third layer features contributions from inhabitants, photographers and artists. Out of the 350 projects that Van Hee has drawn throughout her career, a selection of 130 projects was made for the extensive project list at the end of this book. Because it is not complete, we chose to indicate the year of design and the numbering of the projects in Roman numerals.

The book starts with a huge amount of sketches, at the explicit request of Marie-José Van Hee. For her, a sketch is the starting point of architecture, the beginning of a story. In the condensed form of the drawing, history, reality, thoughts and dreams flow together. Every solution grows from her sketches as a result of a trance-like concentration, without artistic pretentions or ambitions. Van Hee looks at her drawings as a tool for mastering an abstract idea, to achieve plans and cross-sections. As she puts it in her own words, 'to channel the chaos into clear lines.'

The three architectural critiques in this publication each approach a different facet of Van Hee's architecture. Helen Thomas starts from the praxis of the architect and focuses on the narrative as the basis for the creative process of the building: the formulation and the assignments of the client as a beginning for the architect's solitary process of thinking, sketching, and starting over again. In her text we get an insight into the intimate struggle of the designer's quest, a process that is never finished. The final decisions on the design of the building, the process of obtaining permissions from the planning authorities, the construction itself on the specific site with skilled workers, they all are part of the actual praxis. In all these subsequent operations, different strategies and negotiations come into play.

The essay by Christian Kieckens is based on the theory of architectural theses exploring interiors and objects – furniture that embodies the fundamental act of living. Van Hee's sketches illustrate the way she designs interior and exterior all at once, while the section is developed in tandem with the spatial sequences and interior paths through the building. Walls and partitions are not just structural supports and boundaries. Rather, they act as substantial parts of the interior, often combined with a utilitarian function: cupboard, stair, library, alcove. And in this way, the inhabitation is already incorporated into the first lines of the design.

Javier Fernández Contreras analyses the characteristics of a number of realisations by Van Hee, their appearance, the materiality and the tactile quality. He unravels various design choices and explains how they are deliberate and effective, how the combining and distinguishing of material textures is a design attitude revealing the knowledge, experience and sensitivity of the designer.

Marie-José Van Hee usually builds directly for the inhabitant or the owner. This involves a different approach to working for a real estate developer who has a mere professional, mainly financial interest in a project. Hence the importance we gave to three portraits of inhabitants by photographer Michiel Hendryckx, accompanied by personal texts written by the residents themselves.
    Private houses are usually not open to the public. A wide selection of photos invites you to explore.

The material characteristics such as the geometry, the light, the spatial structuring, the tactile richness, the materiality, can be transmitted through the lens of photography, although capturing the soul of a place requires a photographer's more engaged eye. Marie-José Van Hee counts some very fine professional photographers among her friends and we invited two of these, David Grandorge and Michiel Hendryckx, to present 'that one specific image' containing the essence of her work, and to motivate their choices.

In this light, we also include the exhibition concept and the collaboration with artists Kris Martin and Dirk Braeckman, conceived for the *Biennale Architettura Venezia 2018*. The internationally-operating Kris Martin is a former student of Van Hee. They previously worked together on the art integration for various architectural competitions. Based on his experience and affinity with architecture, and their shared thematic affinities, Van Hee invited him to join in brainstorming for the presentation in the Arsenale. The short note in the book is a reflection of this process. Van Hee also invited another acquaintance with an international reputation. Dirk Braeckman spent a few days in Van Hee's house in Ghent. He was given *carte blanche*, and after a few weeks delivered a diptych of monumental night photos. Her own home, which could be described as her 'Freespace'[3], is the subject of her contribution in Venice. The garden, present in the two photographs; two benches, furniture for the house; two lecterns that each hold a book; natural light and an electric lightbulb. The material supports that embody the metaphysical aspects of her house became the protagonists of the scenography.

The lecterns with books were presented in a similar way during an earlier exhibition in the 1990s at the deSingel Art Centre in Antwerp. The large format books refer to rich medieval manuscripts and document a selection of projects with a multitude of drawings and photographs. The publication 'More Home, More Garden 1977-2018', produced for the occasion of the Biennale, shows visual similarities with this new monograph. After all, the preparations for this book and the participation in the Biennale went hand in hand.

That is why 'the garden' is also prominent in this book. 'The garden' – a collective term for a tree, a pond, a vegetable garden, an orchard – stands for 'nature', or more specifically for the relationship between architecture and nature. It is a theme already present in the early work of Marie-José Van Hee, being the subject of her graduation thesis back in 1974, and is carefully applied in every subsequent design to this day. The variations on the boundary between nature and architecture – from the Roman patio with gallery, the medieval *hortus conclusus*, the religious pilgrimage with benchmarks in the landscape, the pleasure garden, to the presence of shadow and scent on porous walls, so beautifully described by Japanese writer Junichirō Tanizaki – Van Hee incorporates and translates this wide register into ever-changing applications. The series of photos 'more garden' shows the generosity of nature inherent in her designs.

In every architecture book some issues remain absent: it is better not to dwell too much on declined projects or lost competitions. For architects, this remains a painful and upsetting subject: so much design energy and determination only ever existing in the archive. In Van Hee's career as well, too many projects were never built. Having entered and lost the competition to extend it, her sole museum building MoMu is currently being redesigned by other architects. The phantom pain caused by a similar experience was described by William Mann in an earlier publication in relation to an unrealised housing project in the Schaafstraat in Antwerp.[4]

In this context, the interview with Colm mac Aoidh offers, among other things, a fascinating insight into a series of projects for bridges, designed by Van Hee together with engineer Dirk Jaspaert.

These projects highlight the seemingly effortless mastery from the small-scale arrangement of the patio and the garden, to the larger dimension of public space and landscape, ideas that became evident in Van Hee's later work.

A bridge is a landmark and requires the same holistic approach to design as the organisation of public space in the city. On a conceptual level, it is primarily about connecting, but in practice, it means plotting the most logical passages for the users. A good bridge design must support different layers: the subsurface, the ground level and the experience within the field of vision – from near to far. This constant switching between levels of scale makes Van Hee's bridge designs a fascinating topic. After all, a bridge is not only a dot in the landscape, but also an object that relates 1:1 to the walker crossing it. Capturing this staggering position between architecture and infrastructure, form and materiality, landscape and detail in such complex designs is a task Van Hee masters with brilliancy. These projects represent more than just a reply to a question: it is about providing orientation and determining an identity. This giving 'more' than the sum of things, so typical for Marie-José Van Hee, is representative in all her projects covered in this book: more life, more variation, more difference, more wealth. In sum, 'More architecture'.

Notes
1 Bijoy Jain, *Studio Mumbai: Praxis* (Tokyo: Toto Publishing. 2012) p. 7.
2 For a more comprehensive analysis of Van Hee's work see Caroline Voet in 'Architecture between Dwellings and Spatial Systematics. The Early Works of the Generation of '74', in *Autonomous Architecture in Flanders* (Leuven: Leuven University Press, 2016) pp. 103-119.
3 'Freespace' was the title of the 16th *Biennale Architettura di Venezia 2018* curated by the Irish architects Yvonne Farrell and Shelly McNamara.
4 William Mann, 'Fantoompijn', *Marie-José Van Hee. Architect* (Gent-Amsterdam: Ludion, 2002) pp. 85-95.

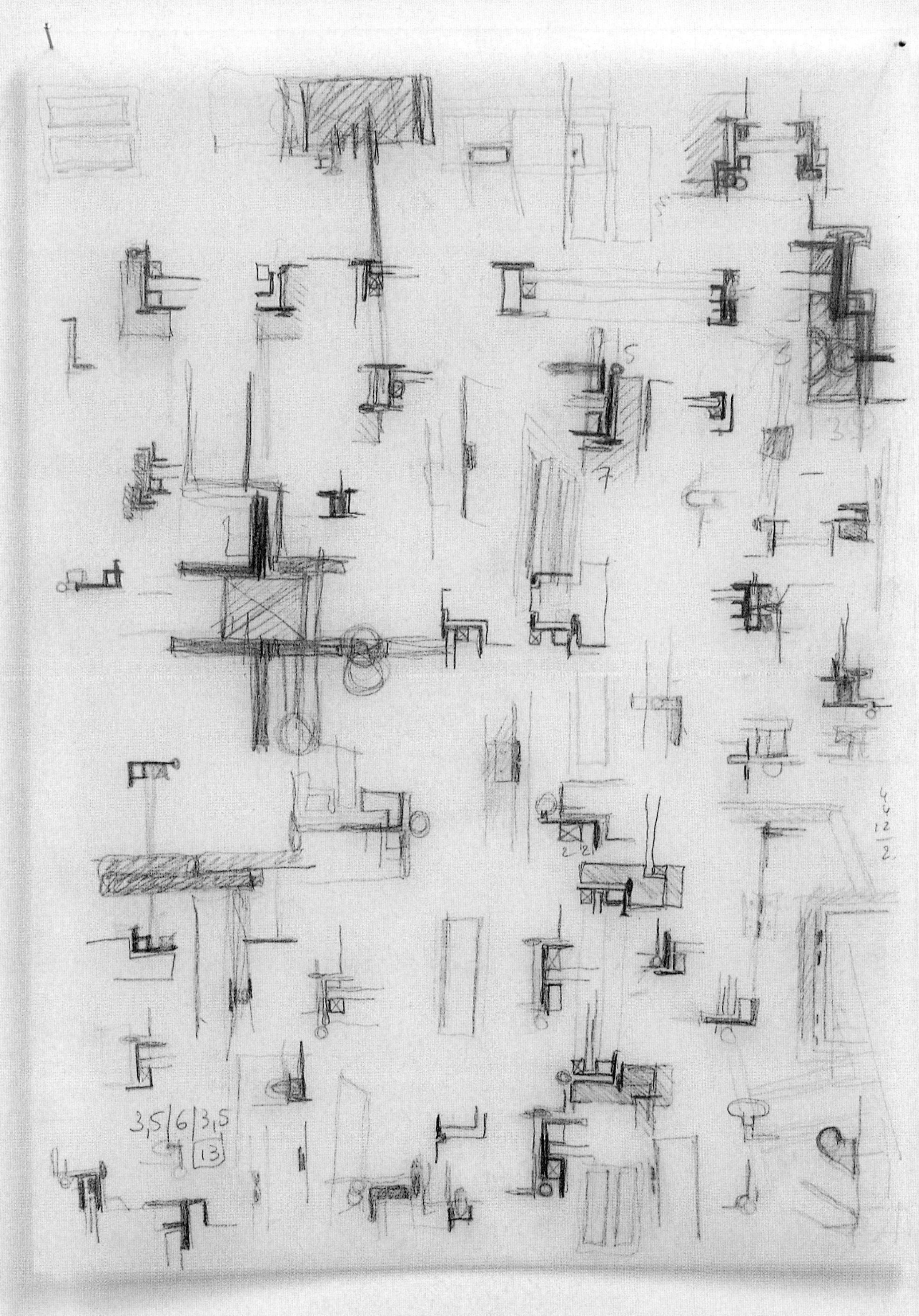

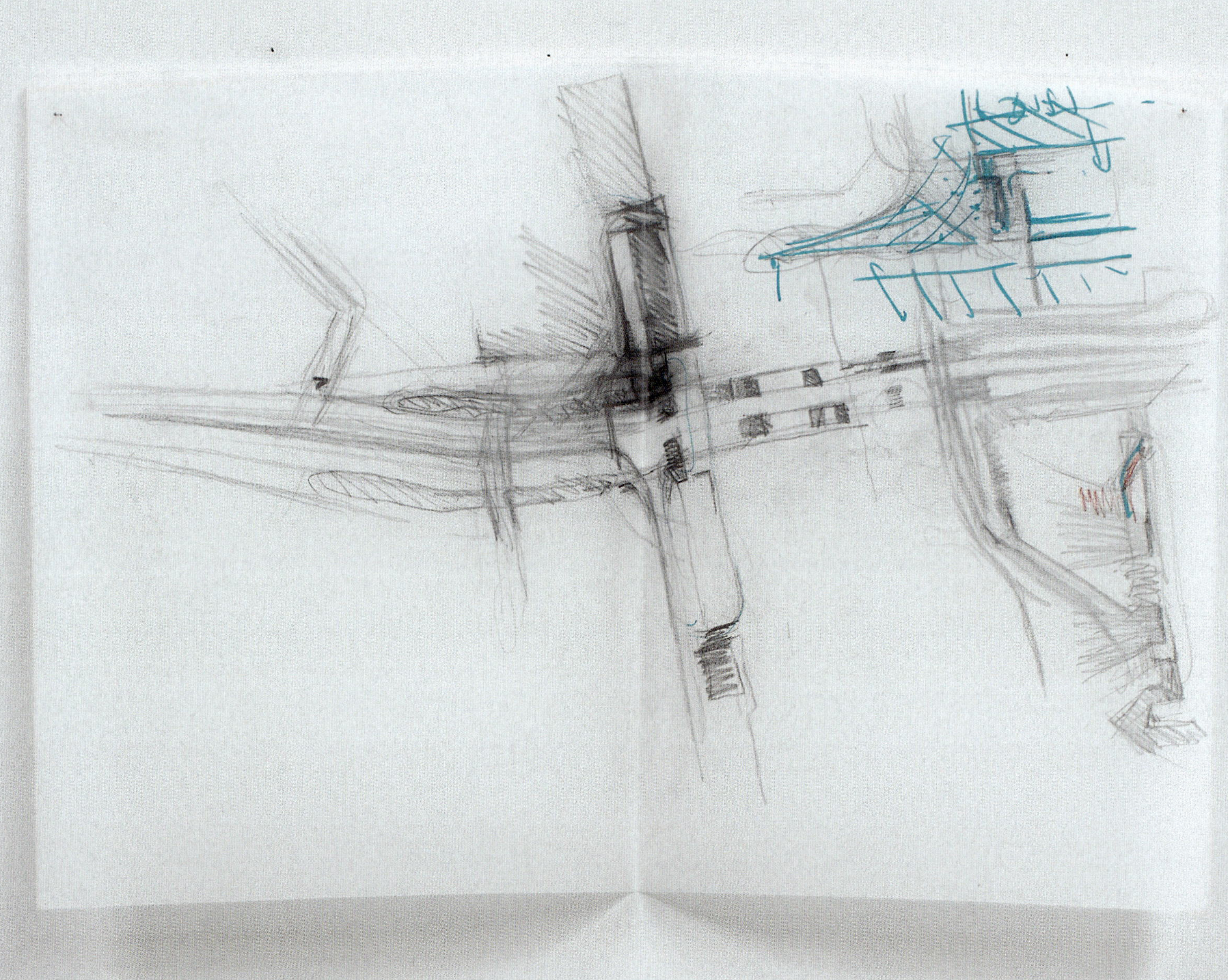

Bushmze

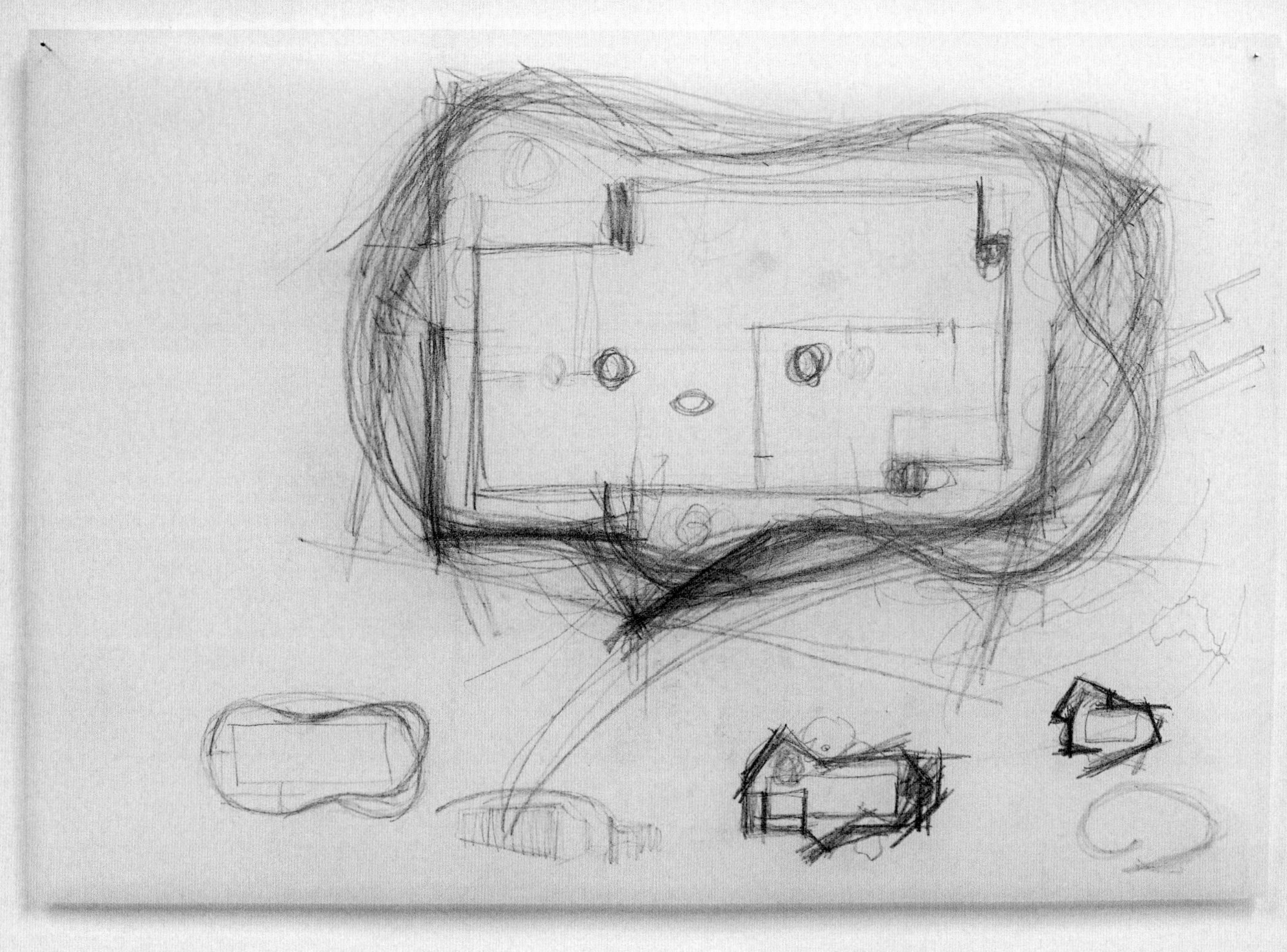

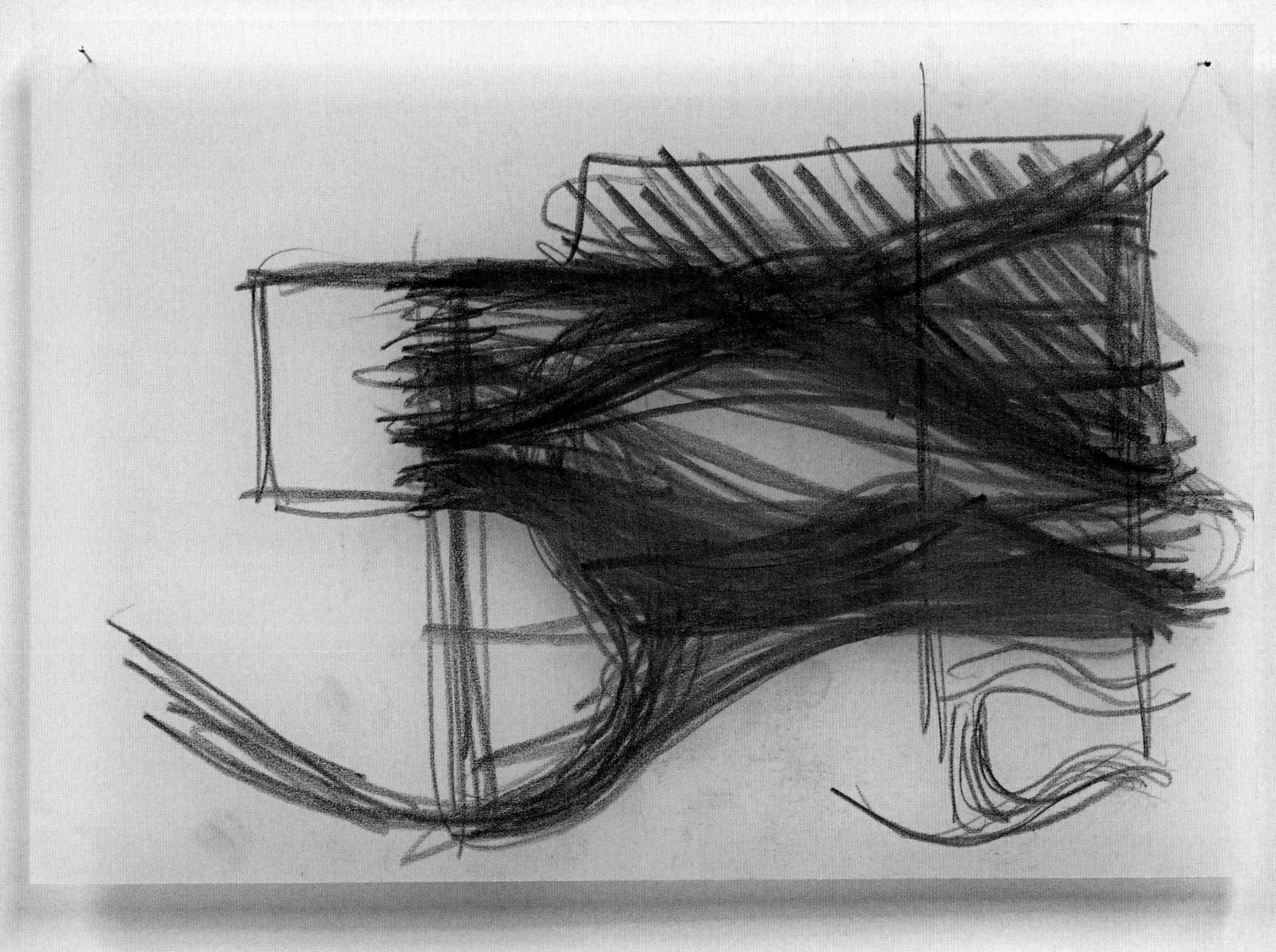

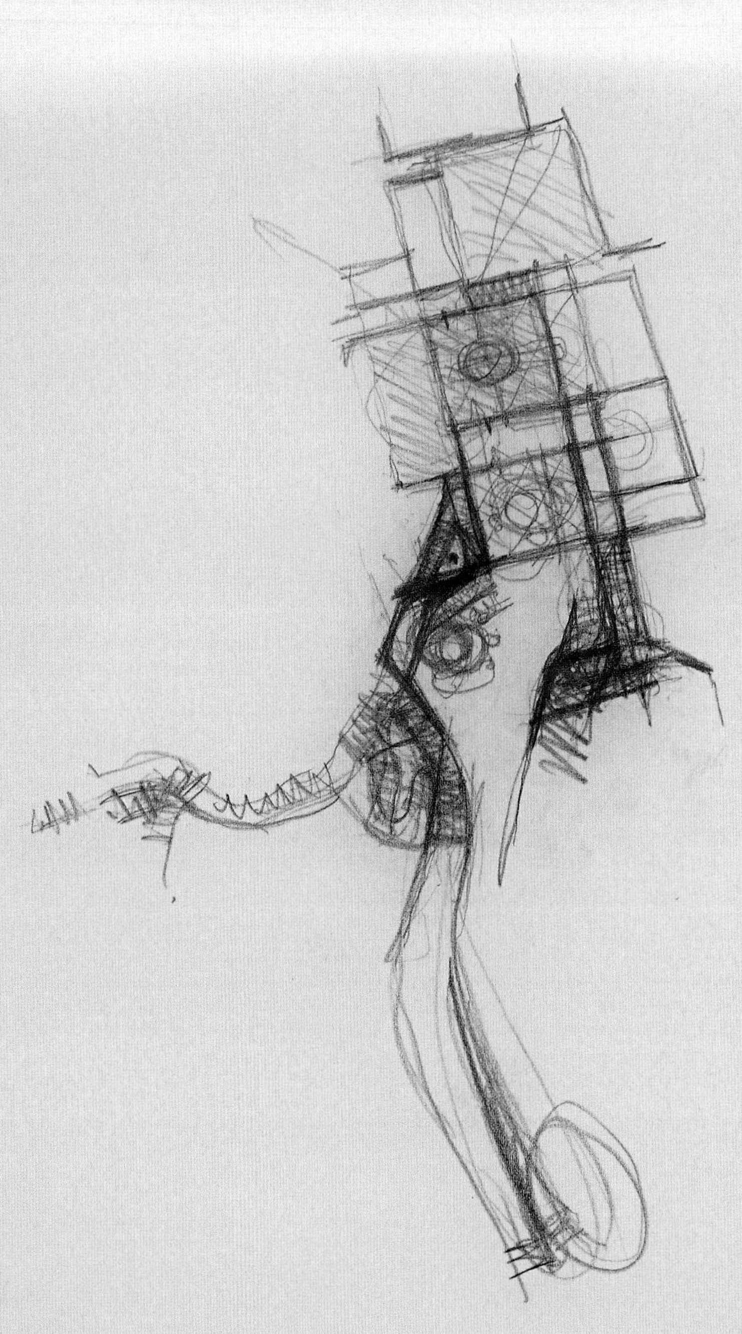

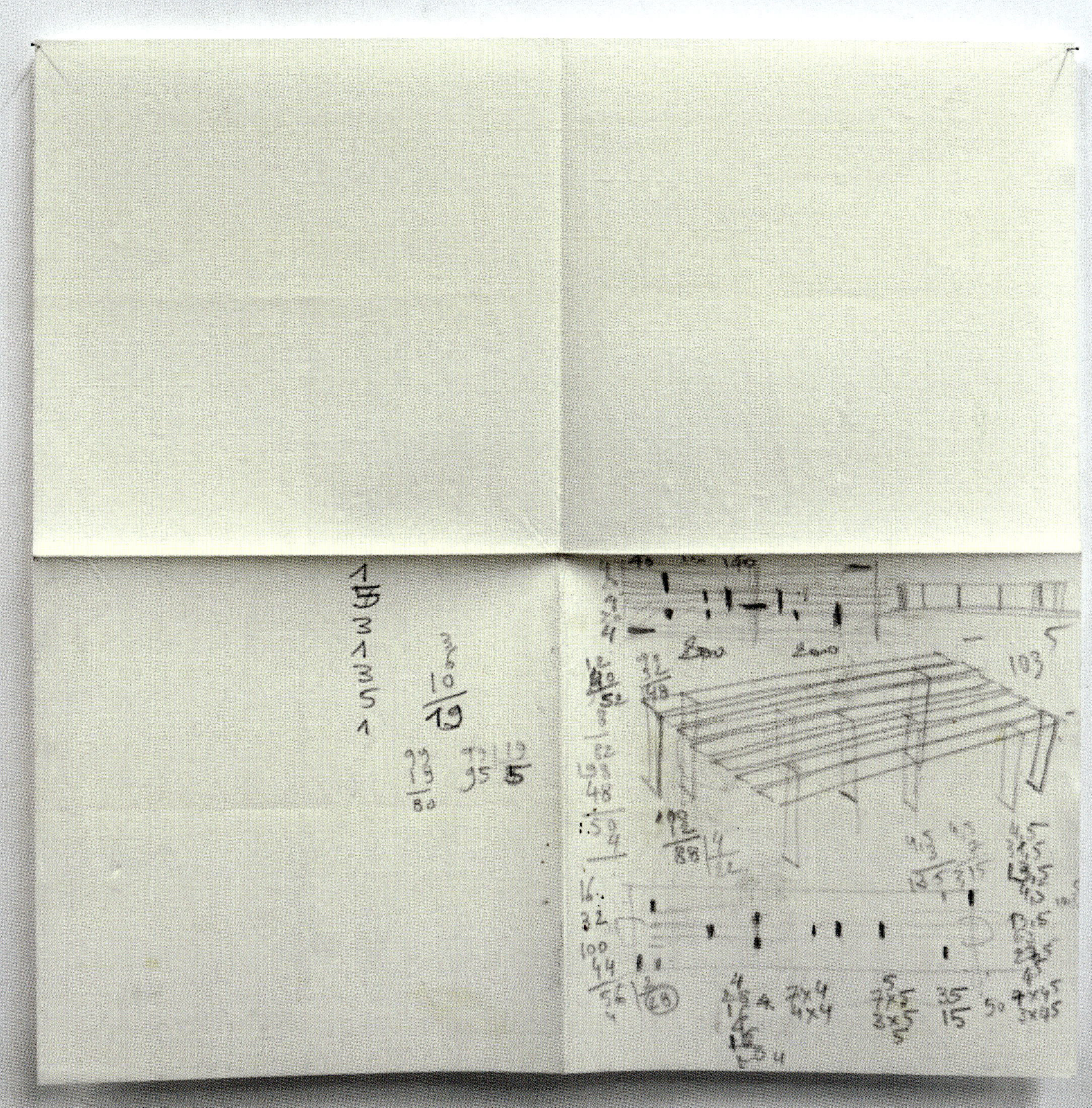

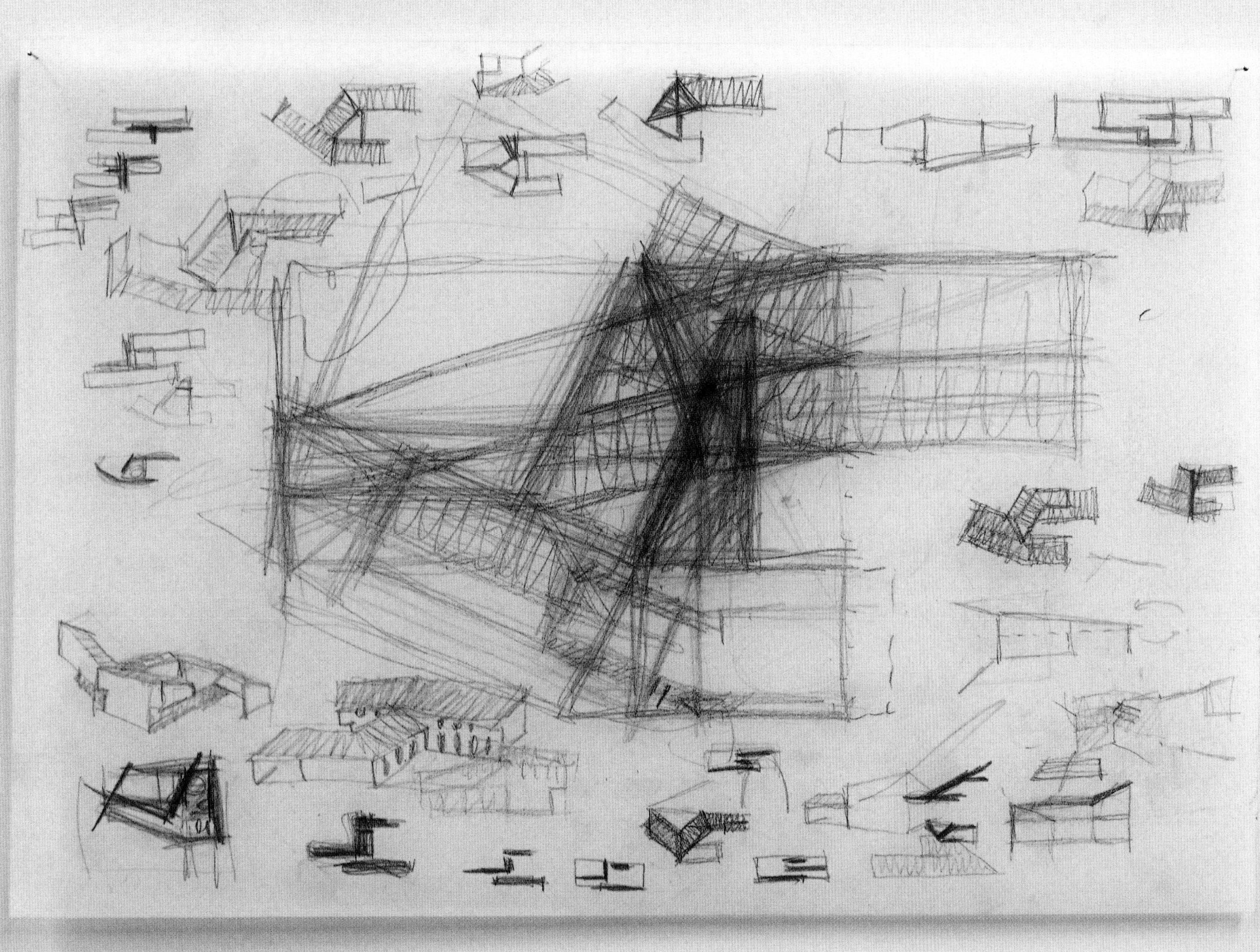

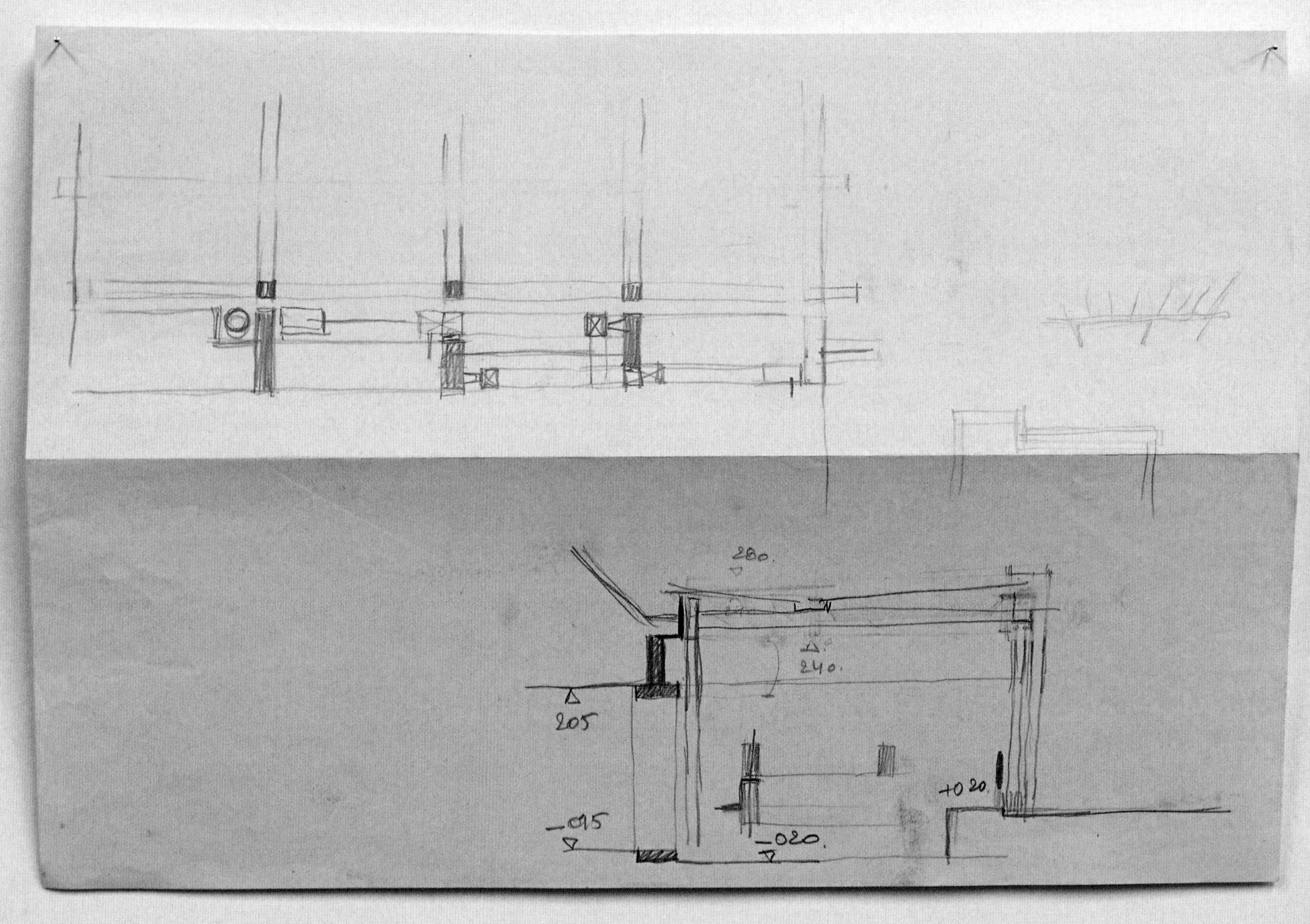
280.
205
240.
015
020.
+020.

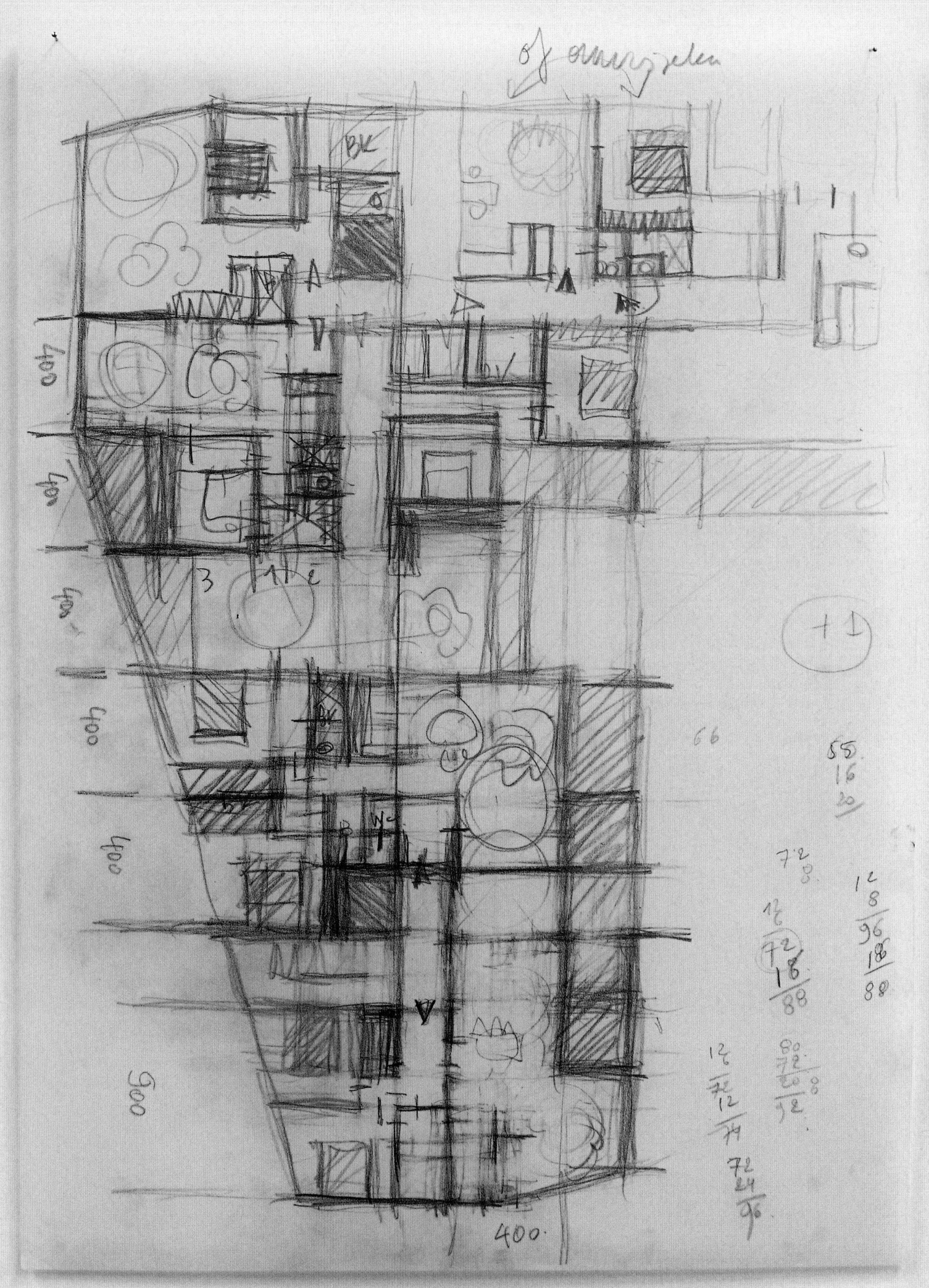

MMXII – 06

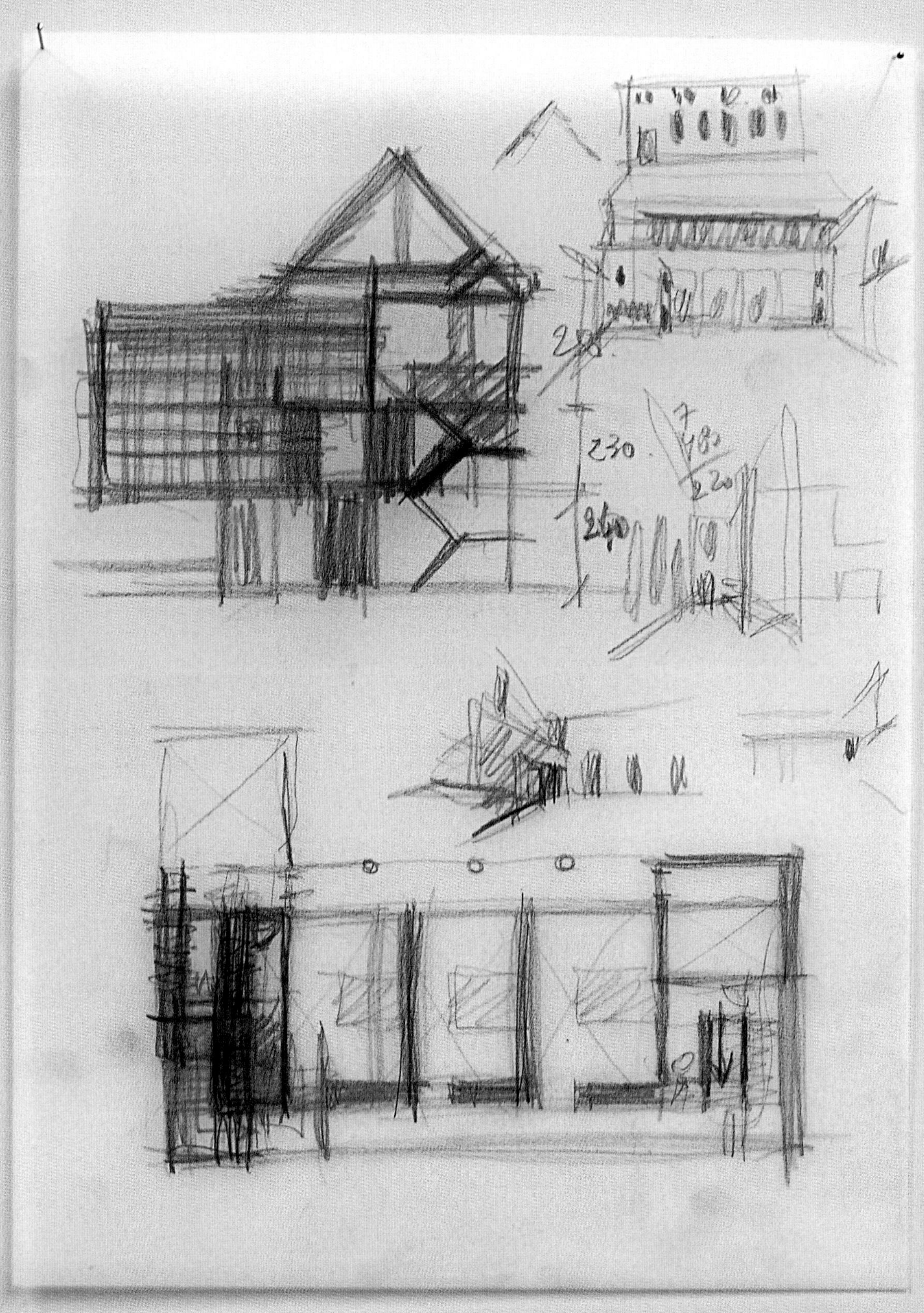

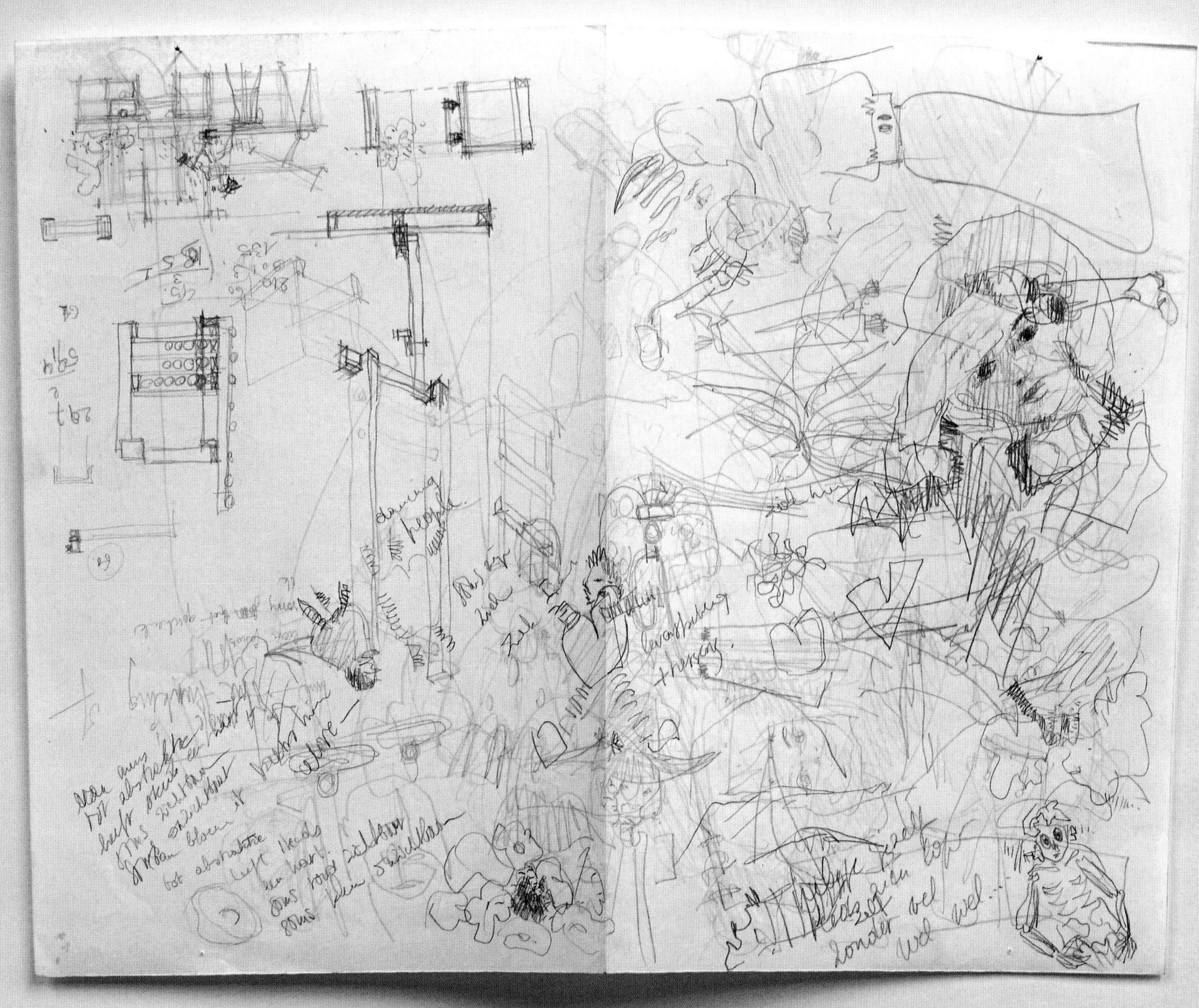

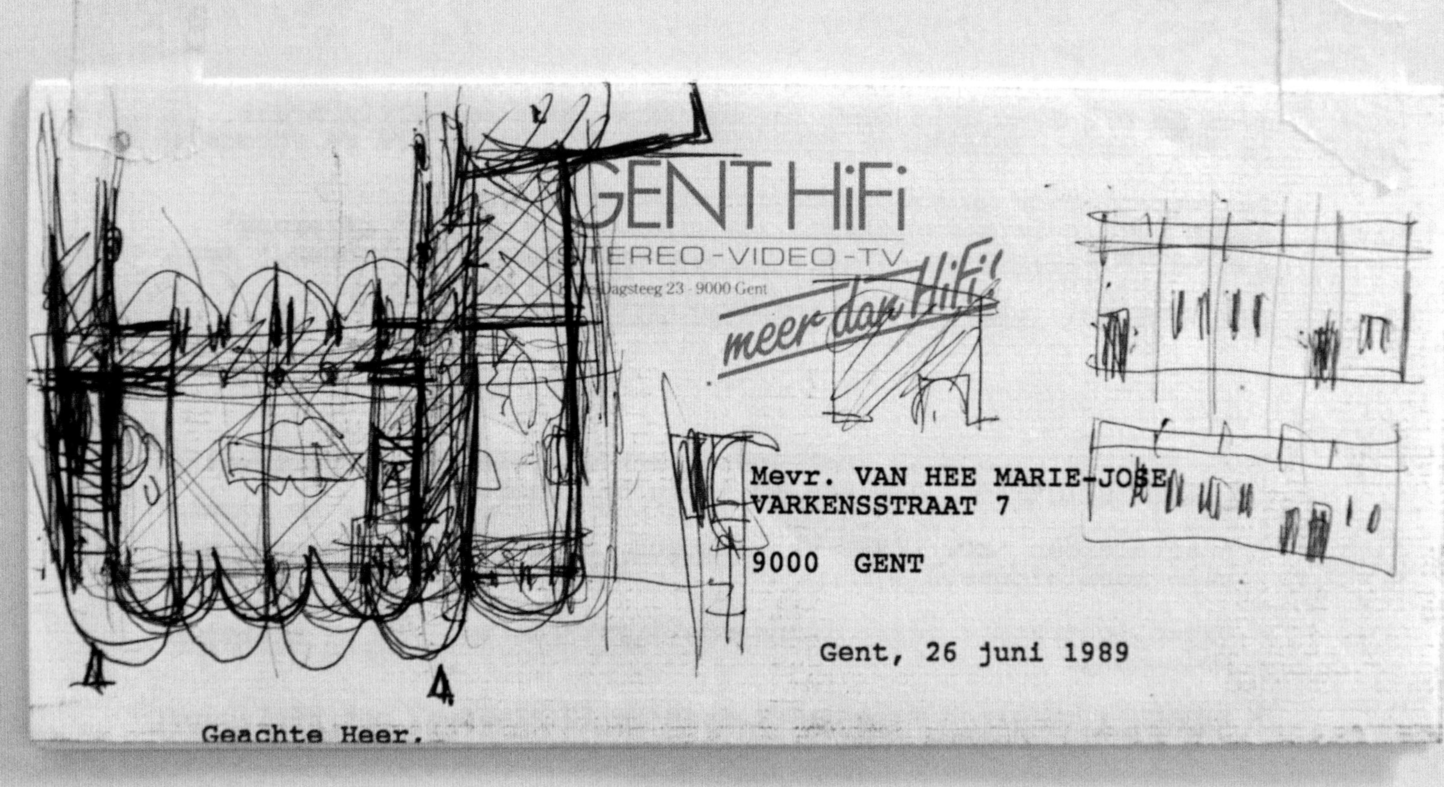

GENT HiFi
STEREO - VIDEO - TV
Dagsteeg 23 - 9000 Gent
meer dan HiFi!
Mevr. VAN HEE MARIE-JOSE
VARKENSSTRAAT 7

9000   GENT

Gent, 26 juni 1989

Geachte Heer,

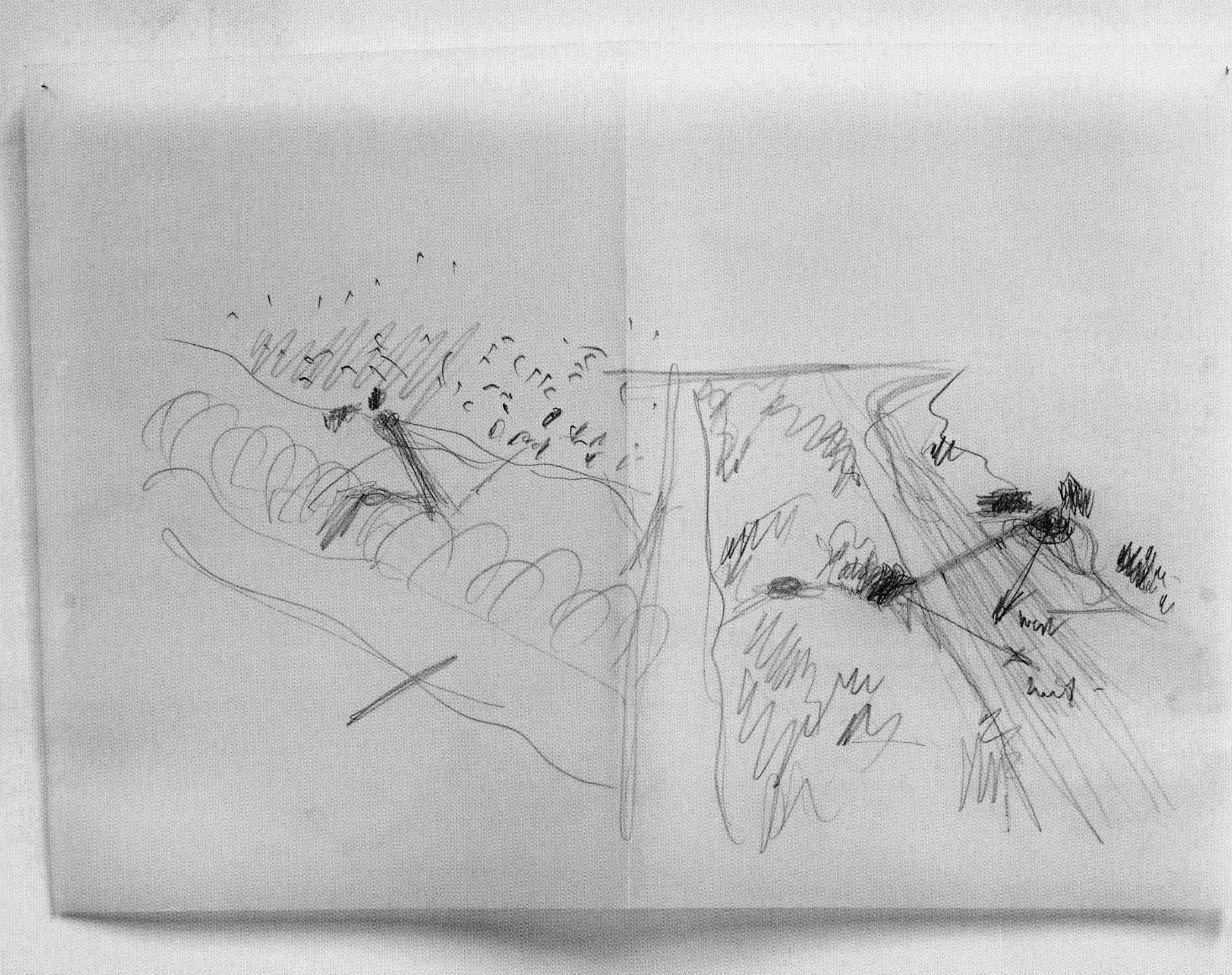

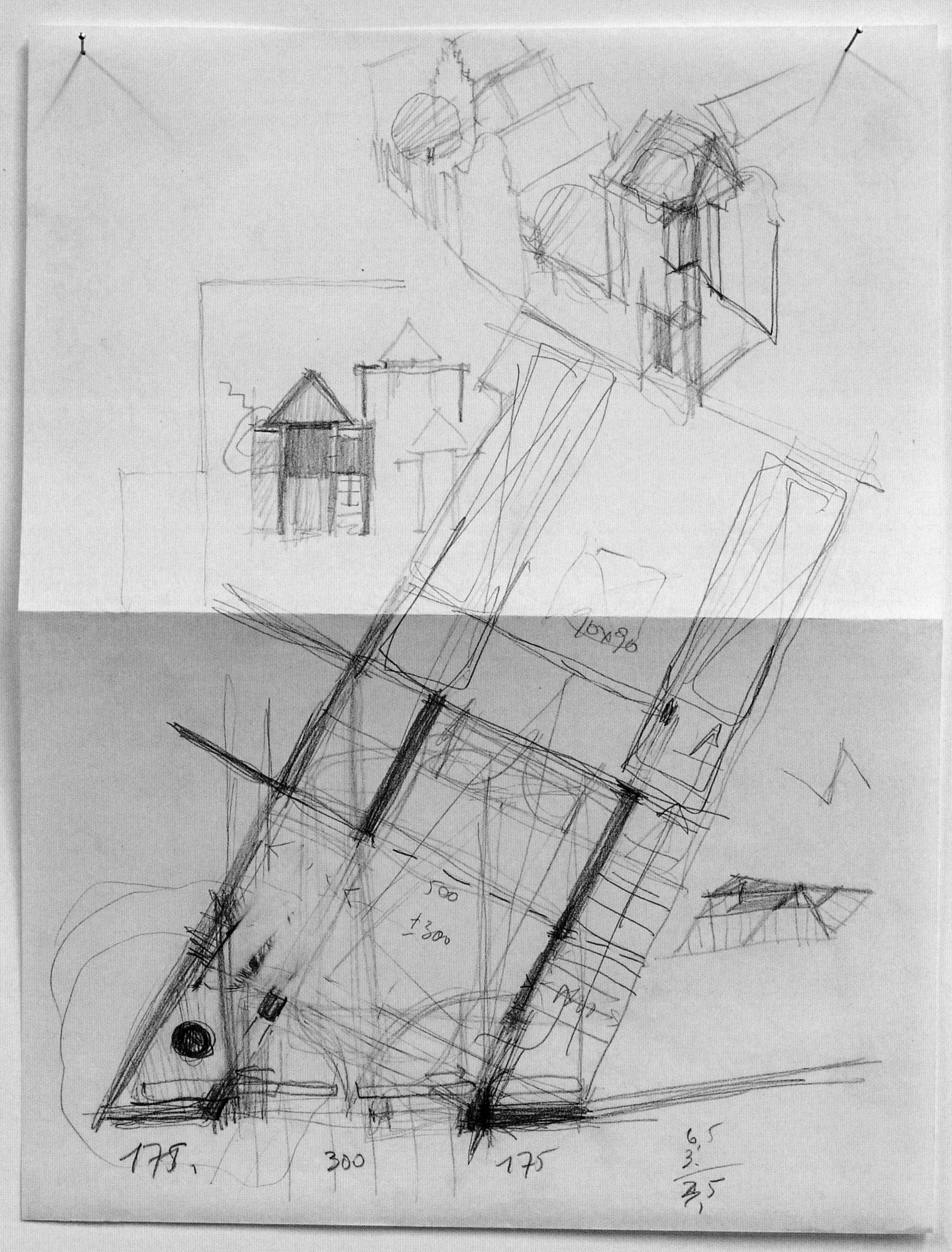

10x96
500
+300
175,
300
175
6,5
3,
3,5

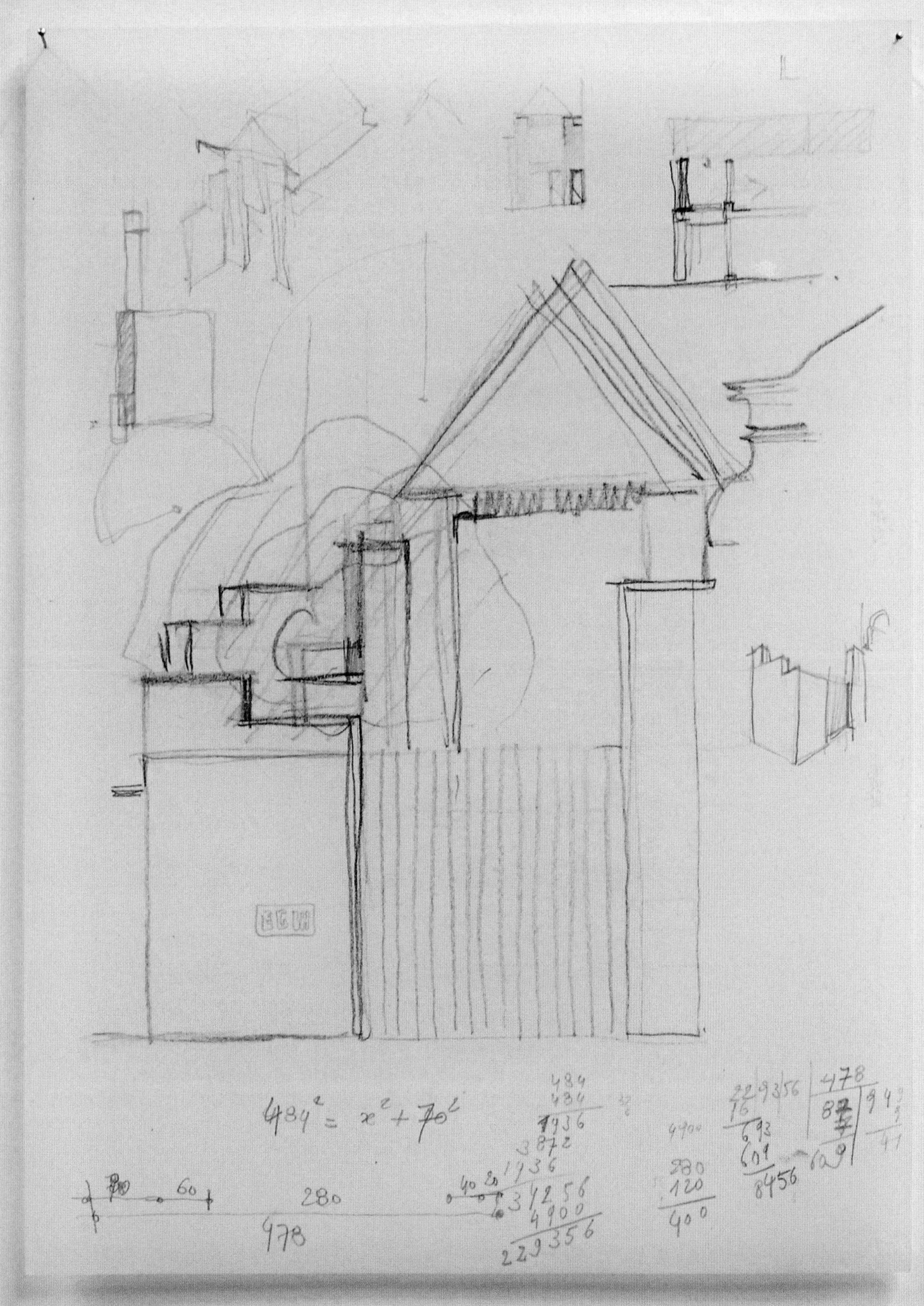

484² = x² + 70²

484
484
1936
3872
1936
229356

40 80
280
478

3 4 2 5 6
4 9 0 0
2 2 9 3 5 6

4900
280
120
400

229356 | 478
693
601
8456

251345

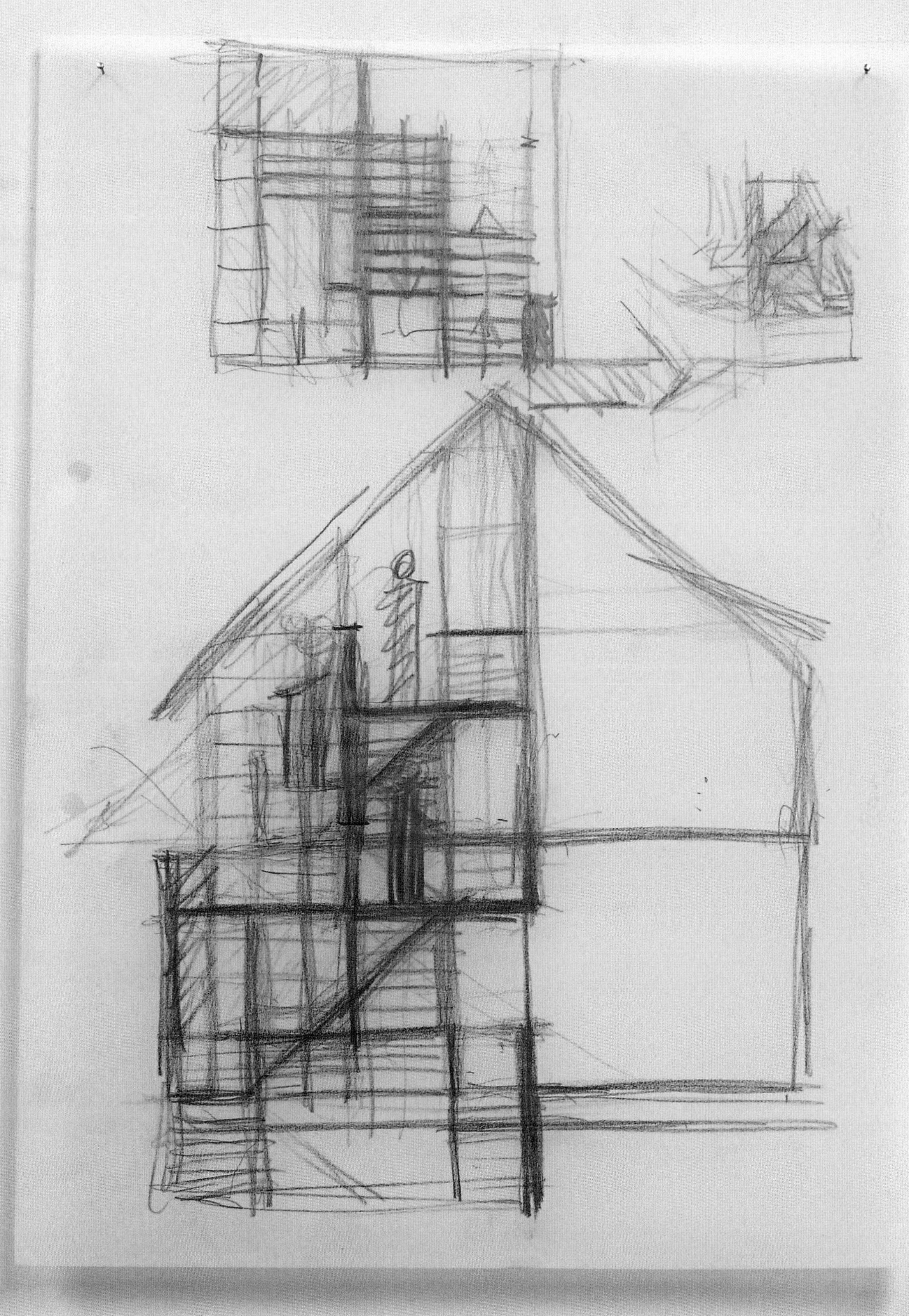

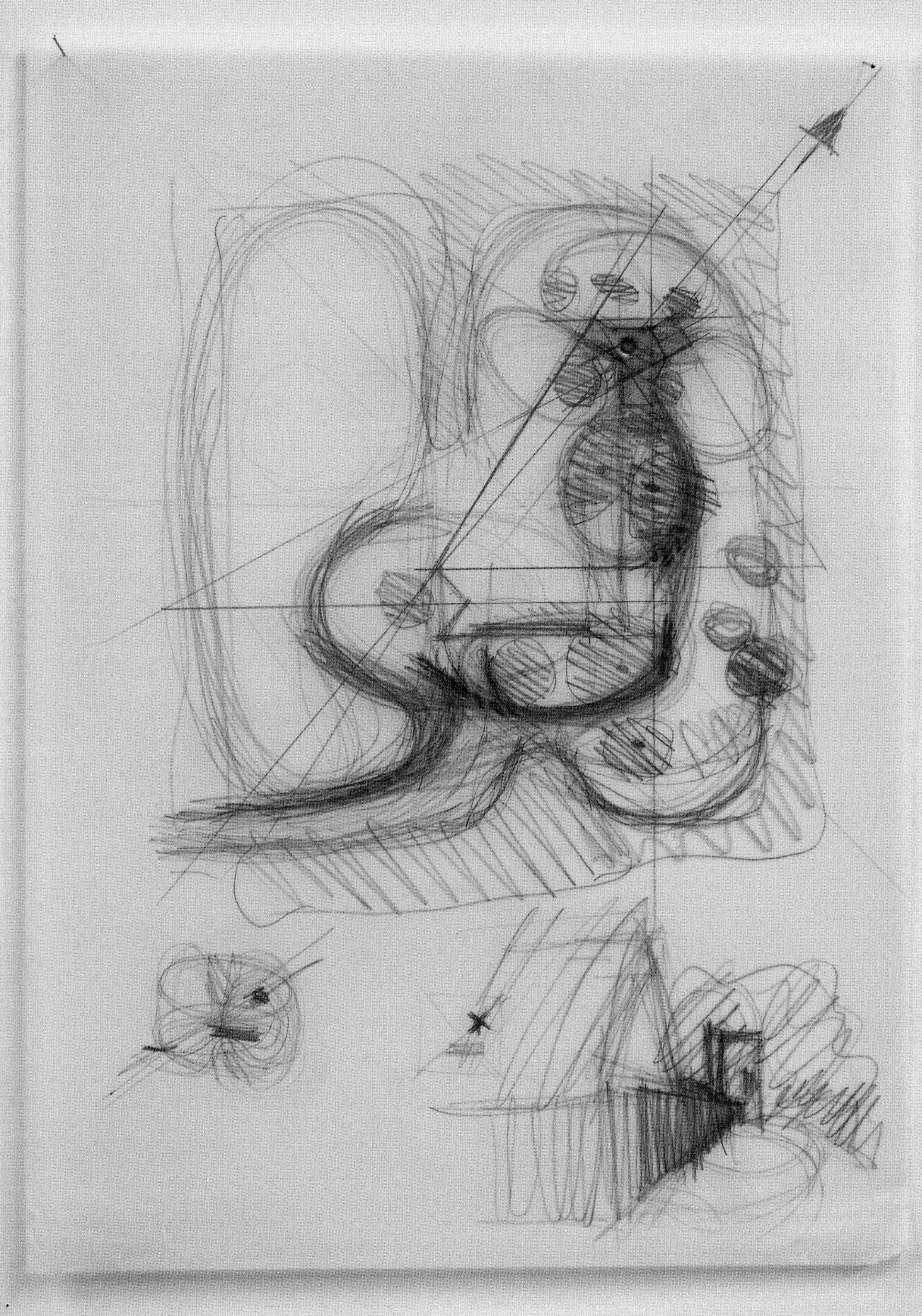

Forms of Negotiation

Helen Thomas

When confronted with the beginnings of a project, architects start the complex mining of their imaginations with different approaches, each one entirely personal. Their way of being and thinking, encapsulated in how they absorb and sort a million things at once, is not necessarily expressed in the final building. For Marie-José Van Hee, these first negotiations are made with the subconscious, intuitive part of her mind, and carried out through drawing. 'First, I try to make the environment,' she says, 'I draw the contour or the plans of the house, to decide what is interesting to keep. All the time that I am drawing, many pictures, many images are coming into my mind very fast, too fast: sometimes it feels like a chaos. The drawing is a way of making sense of this whirlwind, it can be completely black by the end if the ideas don't come out.'

From this process, the principal elements of a project come into being, and an artefact is produced around which spoken negotiations can take place – with collaborators in the office, and with the client. The myriad of thoughts and sensations are a response to the multiple determining factors for the project, that even at this early stage have already been defined: the location and nature of the site, the requirements of the client, the strictures of the authorities, and the sought and latent cultural associations and prejudices that mark the boundaries of what the building might be.

For Van Hee, the site is principal among these initial frames for the project, whether it is an urban plot, a woodland clearing or an existing interior. With her earlier buildings, the locations of her commissions have often been places that she has known for many years – in the town of Deinze, for example, familiar since her earliest childhood. Likewise, she has experienced intimately the environs of Ghent from the time of her young adulthood, where she studied architecture at the Sint-Lucas School of Architecture, graduating in 1974. She has grafted several residences into a medieval fragment of Ghent's Prinsenhof quarter, the majority of whose existing urban fabric was once workers' housing dating back to the 18th and 19th century textile industry. She interprets and subtly changes its formal and spatial character by enlarging the scale slightly with long walls, fields of subdued colour with material presence, vistas into the secret heart of the urban block lit by unexpected sunlight, and new rhythms of windows and openings that rhyme with but do not echo the existing. Certainly the marks of grime, soot and weather, and the colours and the sheen that call to mind the past that made the city's streets are nurtured.

First among her architectural negotiations with the fabric of Prinsenhof is House Lowie-Derks (1983-1986) which she says was influenced by Aldo Rossi, and around the corner is House L-C (1997-2000). Then there is her own house on the path-wide Varkensstraat, with its courtyard and garden laid out incrementally over a number of years (1994-1997) across the site of four small dwellings, one of which she had lived in as a student. On the outskirts of Deinze, Van Hee has built two houses for her brother, Johan, the first between 1977 and 1979, and a later dwelling, office and storage space (1990-1993). Since the beginning of her practice she has sometimes collaborated with

Johan, a steel fabricator and contractor. This careful work with her brother is indicative of the intimate and sometimes prolonged development between the abstraction of a drawn detail made in the office, and the reality of the transforming element under construction on site that remains essential to her work. With him, she learnt to collaborate as a way of negotiating between the abstract idea and the physical resolution. Together they resolved the windows of her house in Varkensstraat, for example. Van Hee had the concept of how the windows would work – their proportions, the relationships of the different steel and timber elements to each other and to the glass, and the way that they would open, which she drew. Although Van Hee describes herself as a builder-architect, with exposure since childhood to the practicalities of construction through the business of her father, her brother has a different kind of knowledge and intuition. This comes from a daily acquaintance with the changing availability of steel and timber profiles, their tolerances and the ways that they are modified, and methods of avoiding unnecessary soldered, screwed or welded joints. The filial combining of their understanding and intention creates an opportunity to experiment and test that brings the finished object closer to Van Hee's concept in the most refined way.

The Market Square in the heart of Deinze, where they grew up together, is 600 m long. On a map it looks like a three-lane road, but in reality it is a wide, almost treeless boulevard slung north-south between the canal and the River Leie like the ludic world of a misplaced beach. This shared ground where pedestrians and bicycles now predominate was reshaped between 2009 and 2013 through another kind of collaboration: an architectural one between Van Hee and Paul Robbrecht together with Hilde Daem, with whom she graduated in 1974, and whose offices inhabit the same building in Ghent. The depiction of the four seasons by artist Benoît van Innis represents the constant rhythmic cycles of the Market Square's inhabitation. His paintings are interpreted to characterise the ground surface and street furniture of specific sites – winter near the river at the entrance to a church, summer with its fountains and autumn making an enclosure, with spring the most northerly, marking a passageway into a woody park. These are dispersed along and diminish the relentlessness of the long space, and at its southerly end, a series of plazas around the town hall and along the Leie's embankments return the landscape to an everyday world. With large urban projects where there are many stakeholders, working together with Robbrecht and Daem makes difficult negotiations easier and less personal, says Van Hee: 'In these situations where there are complex discussions with city representatives and with different clients, where there are always problems and many voices, it is better to work together so that we can share the frustrations and negotiations. We take it in turns.'

Alongside the history of a public space like the Market Square, she says, it is essential to study its practical rhythms and routes: the rubbish collection, the lighting, routes and resources for cyclists, wheelchair users, pedestrians, cars. Their requirements have to be intrinsic to the earliest design, which is depleted without them and eroded by their subsequent consideration.

Van Hee is concerned with the pragmatic reality of a site in the present, but also with that which it has been. This previous being has different characters, combining reference to the literal reality of photographs and plans with an imagined potential grown from memory and fantasy – a science fiction of the past, a fairy tale, that is a fundamental part of her initial creative chaos. This is a personal but also a group disposition. Whilst studying at Sint-Lucas, Van Hee and Robbrecht, with their classmates Marc Dubois and Christian Kieckens among others, dissented against their education. An exhibition curated by Robbrecht called 'Architecture or Picking Strawberries?'[1], to which they all contributed, challenged the complacency of their teachers and proposed different means of navigating the mysteries of (a catholic) reality through contemporary art and other cultural forms. The perceived scantiness of their architectural education was subsequently redressed in personal ways, but for each it led to an understanding of the existing city: not as a manifestation of sacrosanct, unchangeable material to be preserved, but rather as a malleable physical and conceptual ground for interpreting and inspiring the present.[2] For Van Hee, the routes were varied. There were long drives to architecture bookshops in Paris, Amsterdam and Cologne (before Copyright Bookshop opened in Ghent and Antwerp), where books by Aldo Rossi and Giorgio Grassi, among others, through words and images introduced to her the North Italian theoretical and formal responses to the post-war city. These framed ways of reading the historical manmade fabric – which in Italy as well as in Flanders included suburban and intensely cultivated non-urban landscapes within a continuum. Sensitivity to the man-made natural world as cyclical and enduring was nurtured in the slow reading of Marie Luise Gothein's *Geschichte der Gartenkunst* for her dissertation that reflected on Flemish gardens of the middle ages.[3] These influences were accompanied by travels through Northern Italy that enhanced her understanding of Italian cities, and also her library.

Another collaboration with Robbrecht illustrates this shared tendency. In 1996 they entered a competition together, making a proposal that went against the competition brief for a car park by placing a large structure on the site – a large open place in the historic centre of Ghent – that constituted a radical transformation of its urban morphology. For Van Hee and Robbrecht, this move recovered an essential urban density that had been lost in the evolution of 'a desolate parking lot' on the site, which had come into being through two swathes of demolition carried out during the 20th century.[4] After a referendum, a hiatus and a second competition, their proposals were taken up by the city. Van Hee remembers the buildings that had been demolished in the 1960s to leave the car park behind, and they studied the plans of the old building plots to search for ways to recapture the framing of the monuments that existed before. The site was excavated to the level of the medieval city to make a basement, and the stories underneath were revealed. Laid over them now is a café – 'we wanted Hermann Czech to design it' – and a bicycle parking at this lower datum which spreads into a new park. Above and looking over the open park is the plane of the contemporary city, remade as the stony ground of Goudenleeuwplein and Poeljemarkt, whose fields are defined anew by the huge market structure. The first form of the hall came from Robbrecht, like an errant gothic house echo of their schooldays, with two gables mimicking the town hall behind. 'We don't start with my drawings,' says Van Hee, 'Paul doesn't like them. They are too dirty, noisy, messy, unresolved. He has the right thing in his head already and can just draw it. So he does, with his drawing board and pencil, and then we talk about it.'[5]

The roof form with its 40 metre span became more complex over time: asymmetrical, hollow with its fine, folding structure, and mysterious with its layered cladding of hardwood sparkled with voids and a veil of glass plates. This structure balances on four concrete plinths – *sokkels*, as Van Hee calls them.[6] Each one has a different character – two lifts, a cupboard, and a place for the pagan magic of a huge open fire in the middle of the city. For Van Hee, a fireplace is a symbol of community, and the communal is a fundamental experience for her in life and in her work, despite its intense respect for the private, inner world. Another word she often uses is feast – 'we have feasts together on a Friday night' – and these translations evoke a more generous reality and self-conscious relationship to the rituals of everyday life than common English speech can.

Like watching a Quentin Tarantino film; sometimes when you walk into a room, across a courtyard, through a garden gate or see a glimpse in a street of a façade by Van Hee, there is a double take that is occasionally direct but more often a half-awakened association. Perhaps the range of visual ideas in Van Hee's inner library – 'an architect needs a good library' – that is augmented by the pile of books on her stairs, bookshelves and long table in the large hall of her house is more classical and less pop, but the effect is similar. Van Hee's first negotiations with her imagination that she makes in her 'black drawings', her initial sketches, are deeply embedded in the culture of architecture, and emerge as a multi-layered composite of local, western and non-western references. Each architect sees and interprets different references: the hall of her house can seem reminiscent of Luis Barragán's house, for example, and William Mann talks of Van Hee's assimilated knowledge of Roman and Mediterranean houses and archaic traditions of dwelling. Then there is her personal mythologising of articulated references that are nearly always visual, such as Greene and Greene's Gamble House, Lina Bo Bardi's SESC Pompeia, Le Thoronet, and Alvar Aalto's Maison Carré. Van Hee also refers to paintings when evoking atmospheres and sensations that are often connected to experiences of the natural within the man-made world – her dreams of light and dust inspired by Vilhelm Hammershøi's paintings, for example, and when she talks of looking at the full moon through the small windows of her house she can conjure up Katsura.[7]

Responsive listening is intrinsic to successful negotiation, along with the space to reply, and this requires openness: receptivity, combined with a steel thread of certainty and intuition derived from deep knowledge and reflection that enables the final decision to be made. As a person who knows how to listen and when to make a decision, Van Hee is averse to prescription and rules that presuppose how something is to be decided, but it is possible that this delicate approach could make the resolving of large-scale projects that rely on preconception and replication more difficult to achieve.

The most obvious character who Van Hee listens to and negotiates with in her work is her client. After the initial drawings have been made and the brief decided, the design develops through ever more formal drawings and models in an intimate response to the client's voice, who through these discussions cultivates a deeper understanding of their requirements and site. Although the physical form is the product of careful negotiation, its resulting inhabitation is not always predictable, which is the case with a house in rural Zuidzande (House HdF, 2007-2011). As a response to the original brief, the house was moulded to fit a single man. Soon after it was completed, however, the client married and had children, and the tailor-made house found itself used, absolutely appropriately, in different ways than it was intended. Within its compact floor area, Van Hee tended her concern for spaces with an undetermined character through using elements like a double-sided, freestanding fireplace to create ambiguous boundaries between rooms, and a fully glazed wall opening onto a narrow veranda whose floor surface continues out from the room inside, making a spatial and visual continuity between the orchard garden and the dining table. Inhabited by children, the sedate figure of the fireplace becomes a tree trunk to run around, the ivory-tower study for the client becomes a bedroom, while in the tranquil garden only the pond needs to be guarded, and so the determined becomes undetermined, because it can.

In Van Hee's work, as in all architectural projects, the progress of the design through negotiation with the client is balanced by more abstract negotiations with the planning rules and municipal regulations that define the possibilities of a site. In the case of House HdF, which is in the Netherlands, it was easy to demolish the

House V-D, 2007-2019

existing dwelling and relocate the proposed house to a different part of the site overlooking the orchard because regulations controlling the conservation of existing buildings are different than in Belgium. The restrictions lay in the volumetric limit of 850 m³. Since one of the early design intuitions was to create an equivalent presence to a large barn near the house and a visual command over the flat landscape, the required height made a small footprint necessary.

At the time of writing this essay, the V-D House was under construction on the large garden site of a demolished house near the centre of Ghent. When a building has been completed, many of the decisions made about its construction are hidden within its seamless completeness, but in this case the opportunity to observe the live negotiations between Van Hee and her co-constructors was possible. Although each spatial and constructional situation has been considered beforehand and communicated through drawing, a continuous process of assimilation, analysis and resolution of the opinions and possibilities that occur as the building progresses on site is in play. As Van Hee says, 'Between the idea and the end of construction, many moves are made to refine and improve the project', and in her buildings, the close relationship between her and the client who will live in the house continues until the moment of inhabitation.

Ten years of gestation produce many stories while walking around the construction site of the V-D House with the project architect, and just considering the bricks reveals an insight into Van Hee's responsive process. An old driveway from the roadside gate, punctuated by clipped yew bushes, arrives at a terrace that spans between a large guesthouse and the principal building. From this position and from the road, the presence of the vast brick walls that wrap around the buildings is powerful, and in response to this phenomenon a series of decisions and discussions continue. Whether to slake the walls with a pale slurry, whose colour complements the warm-grey limestone cladding around the ground floor of the guesthouse and the plinth of the main building, or whether to leave the brick surface and the web of its bond bare and stark was under discussion at the time. A test wall crenellates the site in response to a photograph of the client's hand against the façade of David Chipperfield's Gallery 'Am Kupfergraben 10' in Berlin.

The first wall to be built in fact surrounds a semi-enclosed square orchard at the bottom of the garden, and initially this was to be made of recycled, giant, red Hungarian bricks that proved too fragile. Next, a yellow London stock was considered, but eventually, following research by the engineer Dirk Jaspaert into traditional garden wall construction as he sought to remove the need for buttressing piers, a small Belgian brick was chosen. The solution arrived at for the garden wall determined the special bond devised for the house. This has a five-brick rhythm, and depending on how the brick that marks the end of this cycle is laid in relation to the wall's second leaf, two kinds of double-layer wall are possible – one with a cavity for insulation, and one without. Following the making of the orchard's enclosure, the next wall to be built was the one enfolding the guesthouse. In specific places on the external envelope, this wall was always intended to be freckled with a constellation of tiny holes, like the exterior wall of the ruin hall at Peter Zumthor's Kolumba Museum in Cologne, but only as it was built did the nature of these voids become apparent. Now they are little crosses formed in the bond, which seals the cavity to prevent rain dripping inside. Before the construction of the walls of the main house, but after the completion of the basement, the master bricklayer laid out the brick bond around the entire perimeter, adjusting and modifying until the rhythm was perfectly syncopated with the volume of the enclosure.

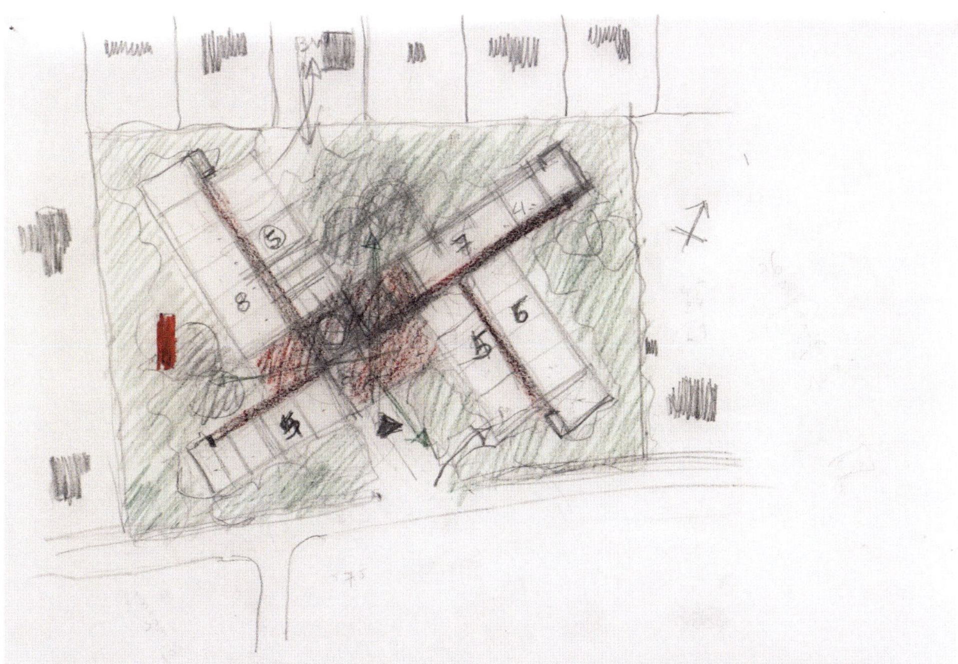

Beukenhof, 2015 – ongoing

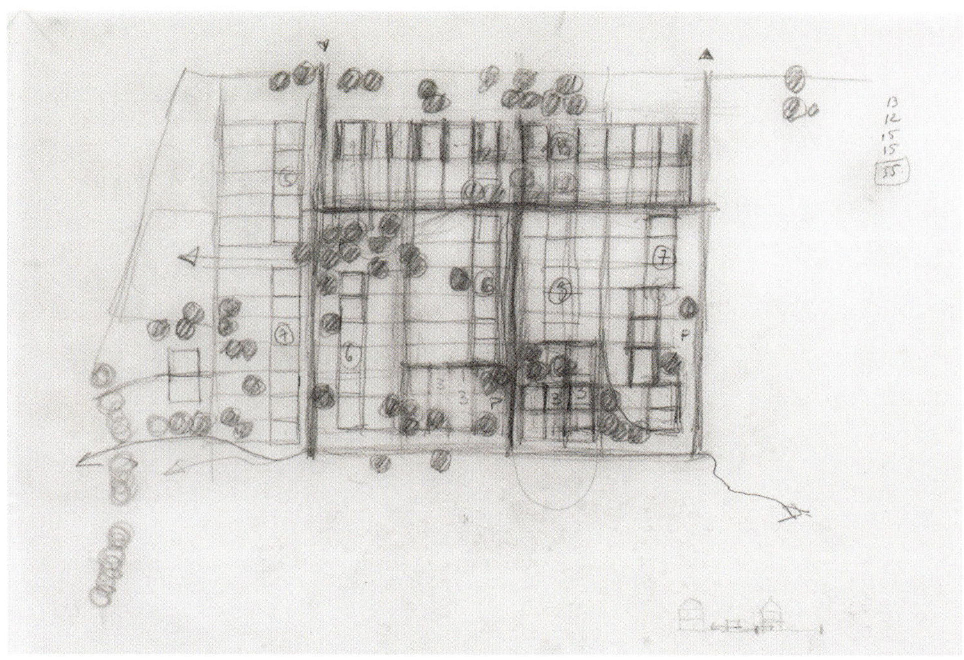

Eekhoornhof, 2014 – ongoing

Two new projects for the same developer were in progress in Van Hee's office at the time of writing. These mark a change in scale for the work of the office, and bring other kinds of negotiation to the fore. The difference revolves principally around the nature of the relationship Van Hee has with client as commissioner and end user, which is no longer personal. The commissioning client is now the financial investor in the project; the end user is many-headed and unnamed, although represented by marketing and sales people. Near the centre of the town of Oostduinkerke on the Belgian coast, Van Hee has designed a supported dwelling complex of 99 apartments for the elderly and physically disabled. Located within a large rectangular site called *Beukenhof* (beech park) that is surrounded by two-storey detached houses, her strategy for a cross-shaped plan with a transparent heart was immediately successful with her developer-client. Handsome old trees could be maintained within spacious gardens, which feature widely in promotional articles and advertisements, and an old fishermen's house is remade as a communal resource. Garden rooms for vegetables or chickens, for example, are created from sweeps of elliptical hedges inspired by Carl Theodor Sørenson and echoed in the sinuous benches for waiting and watching outside the entrance. The building is like a small hill that tapers from four storeys at the centre to two storeys where it is drawn back from the border of the site, never presenting a long façade to the rows of houses looking towards its wooded edges.

The architect and the end user, represented and separated from each other by the marketing intentions of the developer, have different perceptions of desire and comfort. Most often these are manifest in the marketing material, for example when the convenient bench in the swimming pool becomes an infinity line, or the low wall safely marking the territory of the building becomes a flowerbed; these are small tweaks inspired by lifestyle magazines – 'this is what we can sell', they say. Although made for unknown people, the individual apartments and the communal whole of the complex are the product of Van Hee's deep and unspoken beliefs about the etiquette of inhabitation that give her dwellings their strength and character. When this essential etiquette is challenged, then there are differences of opinion. At Beukenhof, several touch points have been set; some are irresolvable compromises concerning the erosion of communal space at the mercy of saleable square metres, while others are challenges to the intrinsic spatial and atmospheric experience of dwelling, and to these Van Hee says no. The corridors that give access to the apartments are quite short, and each is in itself a long and animated room articulated by the entrances on either side. Alongside every front door is a recess with a bench made for various forms of individual expression – for flowers or sitting on, for example, or maybe a small greenhouse, with a window into the kitchen that can be transparent or closed, so that the face of each residence is a manifestation of its inhabitant. The client challenged these bays – they were more expensive and reduced the total floor area of each apartment.

The learning process is on both sides, however, and expert knowledge on the client side has also come into play, such as when the developer added a second lavatory for visitors into the specification, since bathrooms in serviced apartments are very private places. The client's initial solution was at odds with the intrinsic decorum of Van Hee's sense of dwelling that gives the homes she designs a singular character. This sense is reflected in an essay she read while designing her own house (in which the lavatory is outside) called 'In Praise of Shadows' by Junichirō Tanizaki. In Tanizaki's view, for houses 'there are certain prerequisites: a degree of dimness, absolute cleanliness, and a quiet so complete one can hear the hum of a mosquito … of all the elements of Japanese architecture, the toilet is the most aesthetic. Our forebears, making poetry of everything in their lives, transformed what by rights should be the most unsanitary room in the house into a place of unsurpassed elegance, replete with fond associations with the beauties of nature.'[8]

A different disparity in world views rippled the surface of another large project in the office, this time located in the municipality of Boortmeerbeek in Flanders, between Brussels and Antwerp. On the grounds of an old campsite called *Eekhoornhof* (squirrel garden) a development designed by Van Hee for 55 houses, with a further seven social housing units planned, has been laid out with the intention of maintaining the bosky character of the site, and a permeability in terms of rights of way across it towards surrounding fields and woodlands. Neighbours protested when the stipulations of the RUP (*ruimtelijk uitvoeringsplan*, the regional spatial plan for the area), which was changed in 2010 from leisure to residential use, became a proposal for reality. Van Hee's reaction to the site was sympathetic, however, and she describes her first visit there as an encounter with 'an overgrown woodland with some beautiful old trees. I went with an assistant from the office and his brother, a forest engineer. We walked all over the site, sometimes fighting through the undergrowth, to find the most important trees – oaks and sweet chestnuts, and a majestic red beech – and marked them so that they would certainly be saved.'

These trees became the motivating device of the site plan, and in the first setting out of the development the roads manoeuvred the perimeter picturesquely around the trees, giving access to the houses in the form of single lane metalled roads 6 metre wide (the originally permeable grassy surface having been immediately rejected).

When this seemingly simple solution for maintaining the special qualities of the site was pitched against the precedents of the municipal road system into which Eekhoornhof's lanes would be integrated upon construction, a fracture in the logic of state and municipal intentions was revealed. On one hand, environmental legislation calls for increasingly non-interventionist methods of water management. Where possible, ground water should be able to seep immediately downwards and be absorbed, instead of being gathered over large expanses of impermeable ground surfaces into plastic reservoirs designed to counteract the ensuing effects of concentrations of run-off water. In addition, the presence of trees on a site contributes to the management of fluctuations in water level. All of this is subconsciously encompassed in Van Hee's initial creative chaos. On the other hand, Boortmeerbeek's municipal road system is firmly defined as being two lanes wide (7.2 metre) so that cars can always pass, with designated zones for pedestrians and cyclists, services and drainage, whatever the circumstances. Realities are redefined in relation to contemporary concerns and attitudes, and municipal regulations follow behind. Too late, however, in this case, meaning an argument to maintain the original plan could not be won.

The roads on the plan are now 7.2 metre wide; the picturesque quality is subdued and the soft corners are lost, the permeability is more cursory, but the old trees remain. Other negotiations of expectation occur between the client and the architect, and similar negotiations around the supported dwelling complex at *Beukenhof* arose in the detailed planning of the houses and gardens at *Eekhoornhof*, that were also concerned with the boundaries between places. Where possible, the houses are located at the north edge of their plot so that the courtyard in front can bathe in the sun. Along the road edge of these courtyards, a rhythm of carports, hedges and a large cupboard serving as rubbish collection point, street lighting, and storage create a porous boundary to the street reminiscent of the borders of Ghent beguinages. Like those articulated walls in the city, these elements generate a secondary spatial order within the development as a whole. The cost of these solutions was under question, but in these situations, where the argument is qualitative rather than prescriptive,

Van Hee's will is more present in the ensuing strategic compromise. In this way, the essential qualities of her initial design response still permeate the built reality.

The physical works of Van Hee are ultimately the result of her complex reactions to the countless and constantly fluctuating factors defining the project over time, which depend on her deep knowledge and sensitivity towards making architecture. These responses are not always rational, because from the beginning they are an intuitive assimilation of aforementioned influences on the design – the location and nature of the site, the strictures of the authorities, sought and latent cultural associations and prejudices, and the requirements of the client that mark the boundaries of what the building might be. For the final building to maintain its integrity in the heart of Van Hee and to be truly one of her constructions, the trust and confidence of the client developed through a personal relationship is essential. The more degrees of separation between Van Hee and her client, the more difficult it is to overcome the prevalence of theoretical and prescriptive requirements over personal and responsive ones. This increased distance enhanced by the varying desires of multiple world views occurs generally in larger projects: in public commissions like the Market Square in Deinze and the Market Hall in Ghent, and in private developments like Beukenhof and Eekhoornhof. In these situations, decisions can be influenced by preconceptions and generalisations about what the conditions and forms of the built outcome should be, instead of responding to the specific conditions of the brief and context as projected by the architect. Different stakeholders bring many ideas and opinions into the conversation. Sometimes they are provocative and unforeseen, but they can also be clichéd, where something that has been seen before is sought. During these negotiations, the architect must maintain the core of the response she found in the first drawings and developed over time. But this is when the strong character and self-belief that is essential for any architect to build what they want asserts itself. Van Hee says no, and being female, she sometimes has to say it louder.

Notes

1 This is discussed by Hera Van Sande and Yves Schoonjans in 'A Constellation of Scattered Points, Crisis in Design Mentality at the Sint-Lucas Institute (1969-1974)' in *Autonomous Architecture in Flanders* (Leuven: Leuven University Press, 2016) pp. 22-33, specifically p. 25.

2 At the same time that Van Hee and her peers were dissenting at Sint-Lucas, a different protest was being enacted in Brussels by the Atelier de Recherche et d'action Urbaines (ARAU). Formed in 1968, they were against the relentlessness of modernisation and the crude destructive clearance of the city for new development, and their work created the foundations of Brussel's architectural and urban activism during the 1970s, which led to a reappraisal of existing opinions and proposals for the city through counter-projects that were political and practical, rather than nostalgic or reactionary (terms which in Northern Europe were and often still are used for describing attempts to maintain rather than erase and develop existing buildings). Brussels and Ghent were separate, and it is unlikely that ARAU had any direct influence on the attitudes of the Sint-Lucas generation of 74, who were not political in their protests, but ARAU's activities provided a context for their approach. See Isabelle Doucet, 'Counter-projects and the Postmodern User' in *Use Matters, An Alternative History of Architecture* (Oxford: Routledge, 2014) pp. 235-6 for a discussion of ARAU.

3 Marie-José Van Hee, *Beschouwingen omtrent tuinen in de middeleeuwen tot in de tijd van Lodewijk XIX* (Thesis, Hoger Instituut Sint-Lucas Ghent, 1973-74).

4 The press release for the project advises that: 'Rather than just providing an open space for events, they sought, by meticulously positioning a market hall, to rectify this deficiency and reinstate the presence of old urban areas that had become unrecognisable.'

5 This difference in the ways that Van Hee and Robbrecht begin designing through drawing is also described by Els Claessens, who was Van Hee's first studio assistant in Ghent, and Tania Vandenbussche, her second, as one of the 'Observations' in *Autonomous Architecture in Flanders* op. cit. p. 198.

6 From Dutch, *plint* translates into English as skirting board, and *sokkel* translates as plinth. A party is a *feestje* in Dutch (a simple gathering is a *samenzijn*), a feast is a *feestmaal*.

7 The Imperial Villa Katsura Rikyu in Kyoto was built to be an ideal place for viewing the moonlight reflected in a pond.

8 Junichirō Tanizaki, *In Praise of Shadows* (1993), London: Vintage Books, 2001) pp. 9-10.

House Devos, 1999-2002

Regarding my search
for a real architect

Following a visit to Louis Barragán's work in Mexico in 1993, a concept document took shape in which my dreams for a home were described in terms of light and atmosphere. Several appointments with architects invariably ended with the question: 'But what do we have to design? How many bedrooms and toilets?' My original enthusiasm was soon stifled by these average architects who expected a descriptive briefing. Fortunately, my energy was reignited by Hilde Peleman of the Copyright bookshop, who had recommended three books, about Christian Kieckens, Wim Cuyvers and Marie-José Van Hee. After some thoughtful reading I gathered up all my courage and called Ms Van Hee. To my great surprise she sounded very approachable, even friendly. A week later, in the arcade at her house, my document was received as quite natural. A delightful moment of relief. The start of our collaboration took the form of a search for a site or a house for renovation. After a lot of toing and froing, I bought an old house which in the end was tackled much more thoroughly than I had originally intended. Though I have never regretted this.

TOWARDS A CONCEPTUAL DESIGN

Marie-José's design for the inside of the house naturally gave shape to the outside. This is in contrast with the ubiquitous external – sometimes exuberant – formal idiom in the architectural world, which has to hold its own literally as

House Devos, 1999-2002

empty packaging. Just as the inside of a human determines his outer form, Marie-José literally let the internal composition, the need for light inside, the indoor spaces and materials, determine the form of the outside of the home. This form took account of the adjacent context and respected the immediate surroundings. Which is why the outside of her architecture never reveals the inside: 'Never a toilet window next to the front door!' This meant that her interventions were also fundamentally radical, but absolutely relevant. Supporting walls were resolutely pulled down. Several window openings, the gate opening and back door opening were bricked up. New openings had to be carefully created and provided with the necessary concealed steel structures to support and stabilise the whole.

In this way, the whole spatial development of the interior of the house was redrawn and opened up completely towards the southern, garden side. The new extension was also integrated for the maximum experience of the outdoor space and literally enters into visual dialogue with the main building. Many of the spaces in her design can be used and organised flexibly. In this project, only the utility areas were seen as fixed. The kitchen, hall, toilet, washroom and storeroom form a logical band around multiple spaces which can be adapted to the needs of the moment. What is more, this sequence of utility spaces gives a volumetric protection to the street side and to the north side of the house, which provides the living areas with extra intimacy. This flexible design is subservient to the composition of the family and the desires of the moment.

A HOUSE TO LIVE IN AND EXPERIENCE
TO THE FULL

The central space in the house (which originally functioned as a living room, but which has now become the dining room) can in addition be 'arranged' depending on the season or the desired sense of space. The bookcase structure that opens into this area was provided with two large door panels symmetrically on both sides. When they are closed they create an intimate space with a full view of the open bookcase (mostly in the winter). When open, they reduce the visibility of the bookcase to create movement and openness through the house (mostly in the summer). It strikes me that on sunny days over the years the two panels have often closed off the bookcase to give free rein to the spatiality and the light. By contrast, in the evening they provide the enclosed atmosphere of a protective, intimate space.

In the context of the same dynamic, in the first ten years of its existence, the new extension was used as a study and workshop. Later it became a living room and a place for the evenings. Separate from the house, but linked to it and sited in a surprising manner in the garden, with which it is in very close contact, this space offers perfect peace. And there is an intense experience of the garden. On the south side are very large sliding doors. On the north side a horizontal window offers a view of the orchard at a slightly higher level. Each season is visible and palpable in this room. The division of the windows in this extension also offers various framed views: from a sitting position the occupant looks through a narrower horizontal frame. From a standing, moving position, a larger frame is offered through which to view the outside. The dynamic between the extension and the garden creates a world in its own right and nature enriches the life lived there.

The original house, which dates from the mid-1800s and was converted in 1938, had three staircases that served the different floors at various levels. These stair structures were completely removed to make room for a single central structure that combines the staircase and the bookcase from cellar to attic. The basic construction and space are formed by two vertical bookcases so that the staircase serves all the levels and rooms. In addition, these bookcases open out in several directions, provide several surprising through views and include several useful cupboards and drawers. The detailing of these cupboards and drawers is austerely in keeping with the

pattern of the bookcase sections. Going upstairs means taking a trip past and around the bookcases. They open up to the different inner sides of the staircase so that you literally pass the walls of books as you go upstairs. It thus feels quite natural to sit down on a step and browse in a book. My request for a spacious library in this old house with its limited volume was answered by this brilliant invention.

When we moved into the house earlier than intended, the doors had not yet been installed. The experience of the spaces and the light over the years made me decide not to have all the planned doors put in. What is more, the beauty and frugality of the volumes led us in a natural way to minimal door structures, without frames, mouldings or handles, simply pivoting panels. Where necessary we had leather straps made to measure as handles. In this way they are absorbed into the architecture, whereas doors normally make for a feeling of rigid compartmentalisation. Their almost complete visual absence enhances the sense of space in the house.

The fact that austerity and the organic can harmonise perfectly is expressed in several places in this house. Box gutters and windows were done in expressive afrormosia and finished with a matt grey stain that leaves the grain visible. The floors are composed of many different sorts of white stone. These tiles were laid with their polished (finished) side down so that what is seen is the matt sawn side. They form a rich mosaic, a harmony of warm natural tints. The skirting on the walls (which corresponds with the closed lowermost part of the sliding windows) was cemented so as to provide extra texture there too. The extension in wood and glass, erected against a concrete back wall, was given a ceiling structure with a layer of repetitive beams. All these elements might have appeared rustic, but because of the way they are used, their dimensions or repetition, they have a highly individual contemporary feel. And they also form a characteristic feature of Marie-José's work.

In the summer, every visitor is charmed by the atmosphere of the house: 'it's just as if you lived in the South of France'. Indoors and outdoors become one. The historical position of the house on its plot – in the corner, right at the front – gives it a surprising and abundant garden feeling. The old walls that were retained in the garden provide an extra spatial surprise. The ingenious removal of one piece of garden wall, which ran up to the house, enriches the views and intensifies the experience of the garden.

The richness of Marie-José's architecture lies in the tranquillity and frugality it offers. And the life that nourishes the house through its light and views. Light that is deliberately directed in Marie-José's plans and is sometimes even adjusted on-site. Views that unfold as you move through the house. The interaction between indoors and outdoors is ubiquitous.
She responded masterfully to both my request for multipurpose spaces and the express wish to enter a calming world after a busy day at work. The approach to living that arose here prompted me, following her own illustrious example, not even to install a doorbell. The perfect symbol of a house by Marie-José Van Hee.

House Devos, 1999-2002

WHY I LOVE MARIE-JOSÉ VAN HEE'S ARCHITECTURE

—

Her architecture never shouts, it whispers. It does not echo, it is silent. It is spatial and is at one's disposal. For multiple uses. To live to the full.

—

It opens up to its surroundings in a well-dosed and controlled manner. It draws in the light, sometimes generously, sometimes subtly. Her architecture remains a daily invitation to enjoy life. In calmness and space. In timelessness.

—

Her designs literally grow out of the surroundings, the ground, the site. In this way they are given a natural and self-evident purpose. Her sketches, using a thick pencil, evolve intuitively, instinctively. They mature … Her buildings respect their setting and breathe discretely in their surroundings.

—

But the most unique dimension of her work lies in the glorious and singular combination of warmth and pure design. While most contemporary architecture feels cold and hard, she applies southern warmth. Authentic and natural materials that invite one to healthy and ample living. Without any form of noise. With nothing superfluous. Essence and beauty at the service of the occupants.

65

MCMXCIX – 01
Reconversion of a 19ᵗʰ century building to a Fashion Museum, ModeNatie, Antwerp, 1999-2003

At the end of the 19th century, Nationalestraat was layed out in a Parisian fashion as a straight and modern connection between the inner city and the new southern district of Antwerp. The monumental Hotel Central was built in 1894 on one of the triangular corner plots along that would-be boulevard. Following the example of 19th century metropolitan architecture, it featured a convex gable, many mouldings and pediments, and a sturdy dome – in short, urban coquetry tailored to the vanity of Antwerp.

When the decision was made to have this building refurbished by

Marie-José Van Hee in order to house ModeNatie, a great deal of demolition work was planned at first. The original state of the 19th century corner building has been revealed as much as possible in order to restore its clear, basic structure. It consists of two wings, one along each street, which meet in a rotunda on the corner and enclose a triangular courtyard. All the escape stairs, shelters, mezzanine floors and annexes that had been added over the years have been cleared away. One of the two adjoining buildings in Drukkerijstraat, also intended for ModeNatie, was immediately demolished.

Modenatie is a collective name that houses a number of related programmes and institutions under one roof: the Fashion Museum (MoMu), the Flanders Fashion Institute (FFI) and the Fashion Academy. Without articulating them as explicitly separate parts, they have each been given their own location within the ModeNatie building, based mainly on their varying degrees of public accessibility. In this way, busy public-oriented activities remain at street level: the hall for events, a closable conference room and the museum's educational spaces. The entire first floor is occupied by the exhibition spaces of the MoMu,

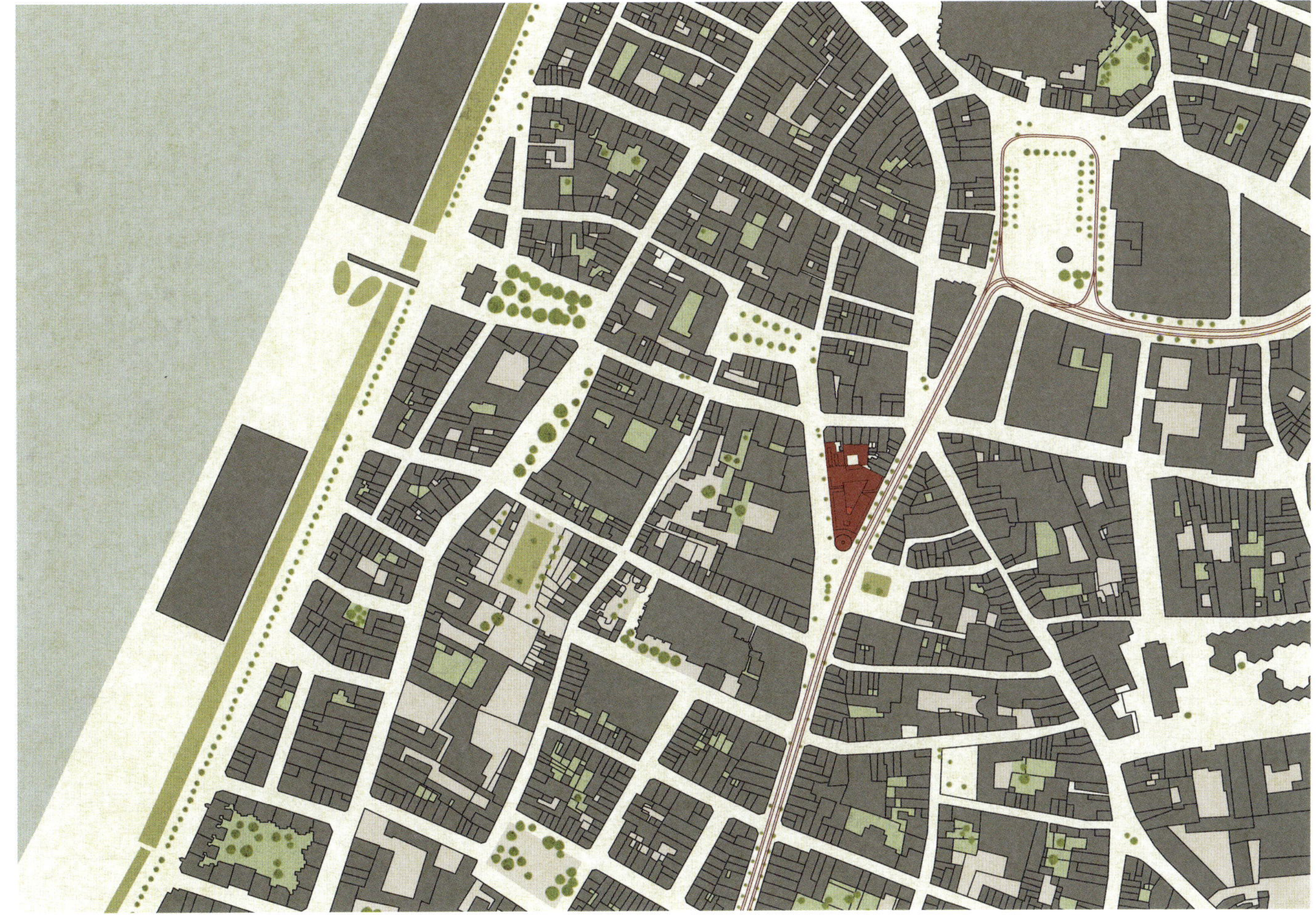

1/2500

while the second floor is less visited by the public. The offices of the staff of the MoMu and the FFI are housed here, as well as the spacious library. The library is a link because it is also used by the students of the Fashion Academy, who occupy the third floor. They have design studios along both street façades and a large communal studio in the rooftop penthouse, where the allurements of the view and the terrace aren't typical features of an educational institute.

In Drukkerijstraat, the annex from the 1970s, which was not demolished, has been reorganised to be as functional as possible. Because of the heavy floor structures and low ceiling heights, a depot is housed here. The other building has been replaced by a new construction with an exterior façade that presents a slightly abstracted version of the façade of the nineteenth-century main building. The horizontal mouldings are straightened out as if they were a simple extrusion, the façade surface painted in the same colour as the rest of the main building. Seen from the outside, the new wing appears at first glance to be part of the original building mass. Elsewhere as well, the renovations on the outside of the ModeNatie have been kept very discreet. For example, the rooftop studio is barely noticeable from the street, but attention is first drawn to a kind of oversized cornice. The fine cantilevered roof edge is detailed in such a manner that it at the same time delineates the upper row of windows. The parapet connects to the roof edge and has a double rhythm of low and high bars. Roof edge and parapet, all in steel of the same colour, have been conceived together as a quasi-ornamental crowning of the longitudinal façade surface. The whole ensemble represents a subtle twist on the classical architectural canon, according to which a harmonious façade is articulated in a pedestal, a central plane, and a cornice. In this way, the external appearance of the nineteenth century building has been retained as much as possible. Van Hee has avoided ostentatious additions, with all her modifications serving to support the expressiveness of the existing building. For the same reason, the bare dome on the corner has been kept, not very charming but a very defining feature.

In addition to all these restrained interventions, Van Hee has also made a grand gesture. Not an empty one, because it is first and

1 covered entrance
2 reception desk
3 atrium
4 patio
5 gallery
6 educational space
7 forum
8 brasserie
9 bookshop
10 museum hall
11 exhibition space

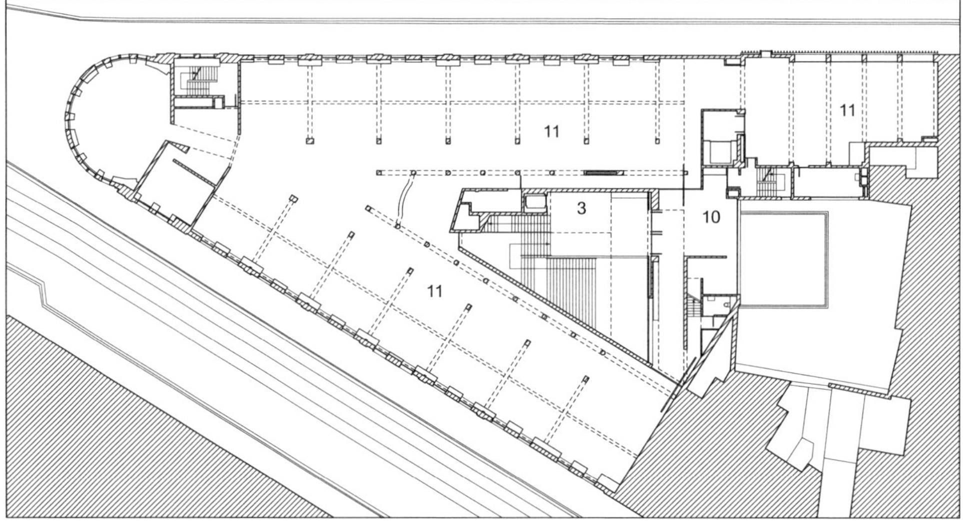

first floor plan

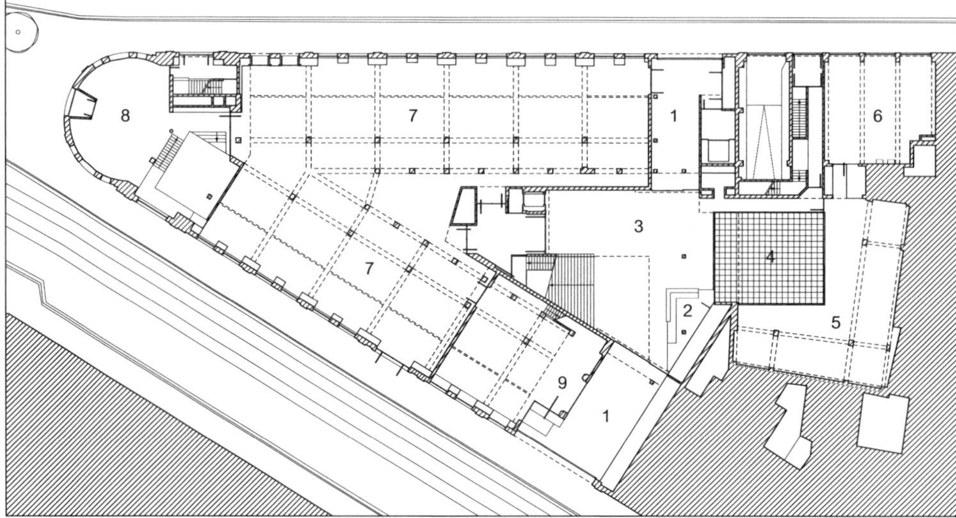

ground floor plan

foremost a valuable addition to the urban public space. Both in Nationalestraat and Drukkerijstraat, new, wide entrance portals connect to a grandiose space in between. The former courtyard is covered with a glazed roof and now forms an intermediate space between inside and outside. In this way, a publicly accessible passageway has been created through the building block where Modenatie stands. Thanks to a sophisticatedly designed staircase, the entrances of all the activities housed in Modenatie lead to this one central space. This atrium forms the real heart of the Modenatie building.

Anyone going up the stairs to the roof of the Academy will get a delightful view over the city centre of Antwerp. Almost the entire façade wall is glazed, but the opposite wall of the same space, on the other hand, is completely closed. At the top of the stairs, the roof terrace behind the closed wall remains unsuspected, south Antwerp still out of sight, the panorama over the Scheldt river has not yet been revealed. In order to discover these other views, it is necessary to go a little further, past the closed wall, away from the extravagant view of Antwerp cathedral. Marie-José Van Hee never immediately reveals everything, she finds that a bit obscene. The fantasy of 360°, of the transparent box, of the invisible façade, of the absent mass, is strange to her. A view into Van Hee's architecture is not all-encompassing, but dosed, protected, mediated.

Kristiaan Borret, excerpts 'De Juiste Afstand', in *Marie-José Van Hee. Architect* (Gent-Amsterdam: Ludion, 2002) pp. 96-107.

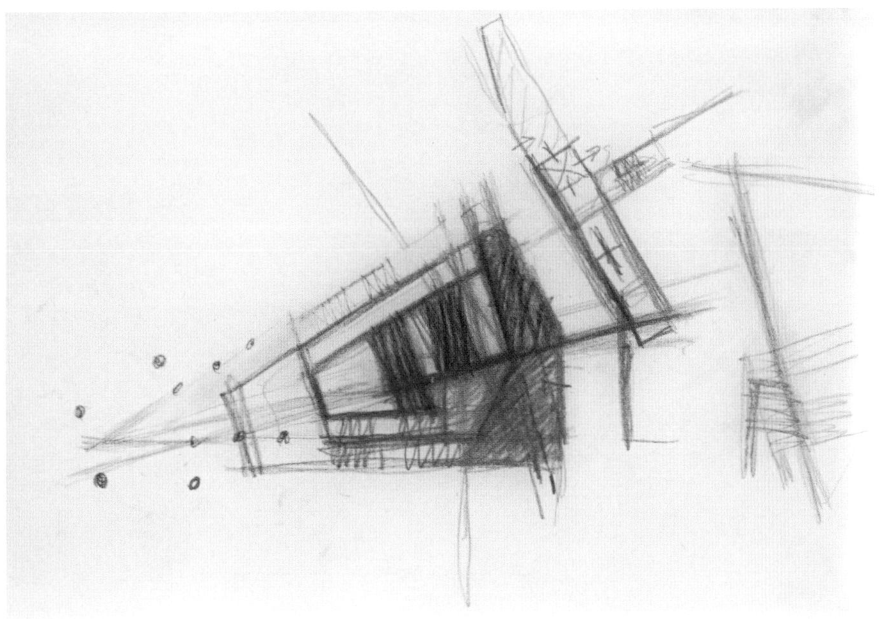

House Van Leemput – Oosterlinck, Wetteren, 2000-2003

The owner of a furniture store that Marie-José Van Hee had converted in the centre of Wetteren once again approached her to design an adjoining house for his daughter, with a self-contained elderly apartment.

The site for the dwelling, as deep as that of the commercial building, presented a number of particular, not so favourable conditions. By elevating the site for the apartment and situating the main house on the upper level, the architect has managed to work around these burdensome constraints, with an attractive urban home as the result. The high walls around the site have been neutralised by the addition of a raised wooden walkway, while on the opposite side, a covered concrete passageway for private cars and the right of access easement lies on a lower level than the garden and living areas.

The L-shaped floor plan places the bedrooms along a corridor in the longer wing, which is set back somewhat from the party wall in order to allow abundant natural light to flow both inside and to the passageway below, as well as to the neighbouring building.

This is a strategy that has been employed by Van Hee in other projects to the same effect – for example at Bailleul in Ghent, where a similar setback from the neighbouring building creates a passage at ground level, and on the first floor brings natural light into the bathroom and corridor in the sleeping quarters; and at House L-C in Ghent, where as well as providing a path to the backyard, it allows the sunlight to penetrate deep into the house, with the evening sun permeating the living area on the first floor in unexpected ways.

The living room and kitchen, with a large roof light above the worktop, is located on the shorter side. The kink in the street façade gives rise to a balcony between the living

1/2500

room and the street. This kink has been cleverly absorbed by a tripartite folding of the front elevation: the ground floor façade, the edge of the balcony and roof, and the first floor façade all meet the street at slightly different angles in order to align the house with the neighbouring buildings on either side. Circulation via terraces, a gangway, steps, large and smaller staircases make possible different routes and future alternative use of the spaces. The elevated, south oriented garden is the central figure around which the whole house and apartment are conceived; here, at the suggestion of the architect, a plane tree has been planted.

Van Hee would go on to build two more houses for this family: the house and doctor's practice Van Aelten – Oosterlinck (p. 205) near Brussels in Opwijk, and one in the same street as the parents' home, on the opposite side of the shop. In a typical Flemish street – a thoroughfare leading to the centre – these three adjoining buildings form a striking unity through their material, colour and façade construction. A shared primary materiality of massive limestone block masonry ensures that the three volumes are read as one continuous, coherent ensemble. Wood and steel joinery and steel balustrades in varying shades of grey subtly distinguish the three façades, and introduce vertical elements that expand and contract across the horizontal composition.

The other projects mentioned in this text are MCMXCVII – 02 and MMIII – 02.

1 entrance
2 living area
3 kitchen
4 shower room
5 gallery
6 courtyard
7 bedroom
8 garden
9 terrace
10 bathroom
11 technical room
12 laundry & storage

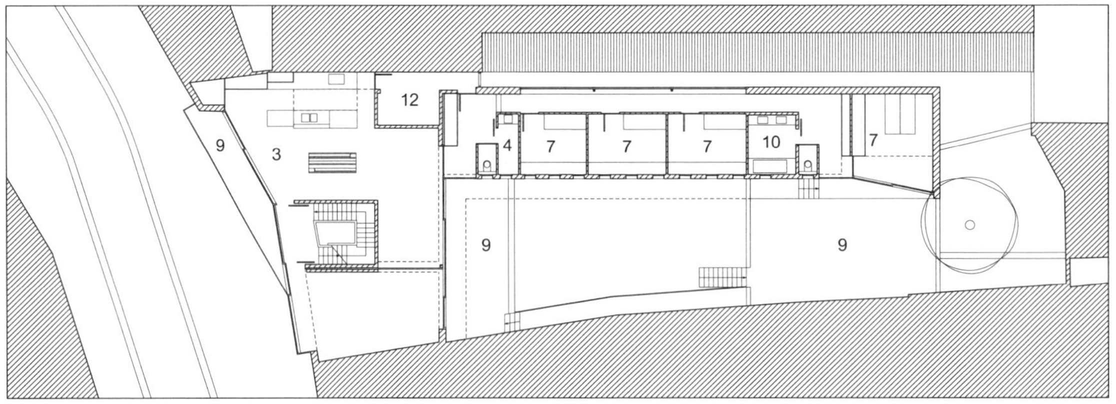

first floor plan

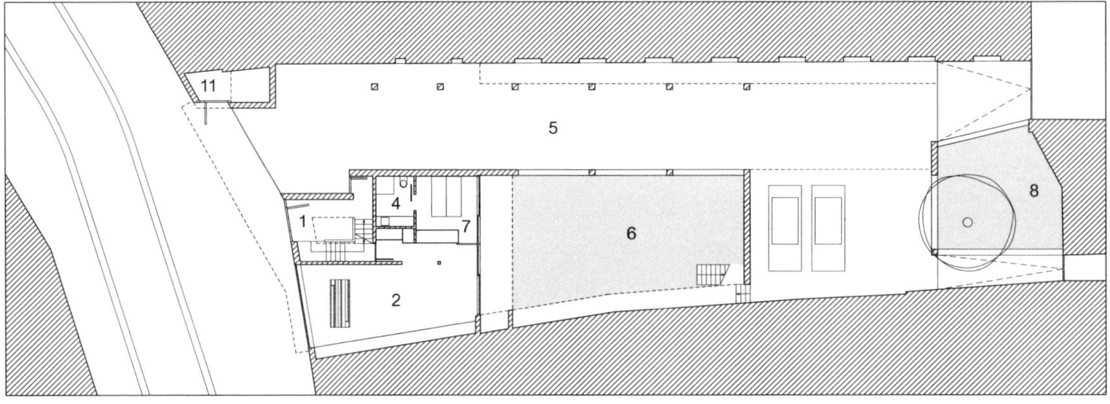

ground floor plan

0 1 3 5 m

Situated within walking distance of Sint-Pieters station in Ghent, this combined office and residence forms part of a relatively large urban block along the railway line. The busyness and noise of the street is in stark contrast to the peace and leafy verdure within the interior of the block. Integrating the double building programme of home and office on the site proved challenging. The design of the building is the condensation of a durable concept and a twofold programme into a dual context, with a structure that is adaptable over time, a quality shared with many late 19th and early 20th century Belgian townhouses.

The desire of the client to work surrounded by greenery formed the starting point for the office. Inside the elongated plot that narrows somewhat towards the rear, a modular steel structure was erected, a glazed pavilion that refers to a pergola or a colonnade in a park. This steel structure stands on an underground concrete basin, with I-shaped steel trusses carrying a suspended roof and ceiling. Daylight washes into the underground archive through the exterior glass walls along the stairwell, which act as clerestory windows for the basement. In certain places along the pavilion, careful shifting of

the glazed walls has formed interstitial outdoor spaces. The creation of these 'secret gardens' divides the office into zones, each with a specific view of their own outdoor spaces. Working amongst these areas of greenery, observing the growth and dynamics of the plants throughout the seasons, offers a special luxury in the inorganic, man-made context of the city.

The structural idea for the office building has grown out of a desire to provide flexibility of use over time, and allows possible future uses for both the concrete basin and the steel structure, whether or not the glass

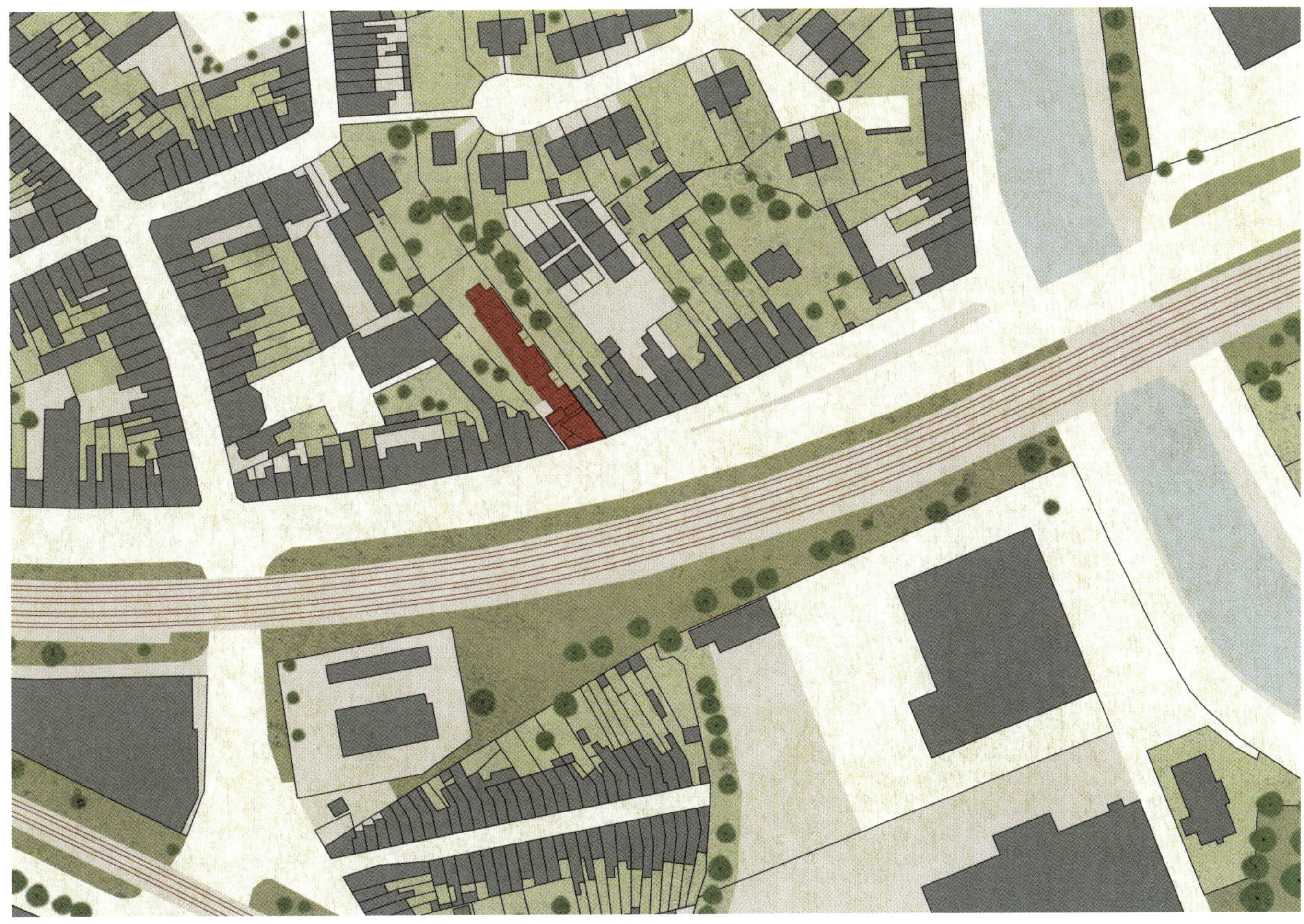

1/2500

walls and the roof are removed. A large, continuous garden is the ultimate intended future, with the concrete basin filled with water to become a pond or swimming pool, and the open pergola structure becoming overgrown with greenery.

The residential component is situated on the perimeter of the site along the streetfront, and in contrast to the office is more solid in character. This solidity, achieved through the use of concrete, natural stone and exterior plastering, absorbs the hustle and bustle of the street. A tall, covered passageway connects the street to the office, and hence also the inner gardens.

Instead of building directly against the neighbouring property on the left-hand side, a conscious decision has been made to step the house away from the party wall, by a distance of just over a metre. This setback allows sunlight to filter through the gap between the buildings and enter both the house and the passageway below, enabling the architect to provide natural light to the bathroom and corridor in the sleeping quarters, while still respecting the private nature of these areas, a solution that echoes other projects by Van Hee.

By the same token, a meeting room at the centre of the first floor ingeniously receives daylight via a skeletal framed light well that connects the solid volume of the house to the pavilion structure of the office, with this light supplemented by an internal window on the side of the street.

Positioning the dwelling above the office component ensures that the inhabitants are afforded the necessary privacy, and, being higher up, they enjoy views both towards the city and over the railway tracks. The entrance to the house folds back into the façade. Once inside, a route along several staircases leads, via the private chambers containing bedrooms and bathrooms, to a high living space with a view of three church towers on the upper level. The sitting area overlooks the lower dining room, and opens out through two large sliding windows onto a covered outdoor area, and a northern and southern terrace. The plant-covered roof and verdant outdoor spaces of the office reinforce the green and leafy character of the interior of the block.

1 covered exterior
2 parking / bicycle storage
3 private entrance
4 entrance
5 reception
6 meeting room
7 office
8 printroom
9 landscape office
10 kitchen
11 dining room
12 basement / archive
13 terrace
14 garden
15 green roof
16 bathroom
17 bedroom
18 storage
19 seating area

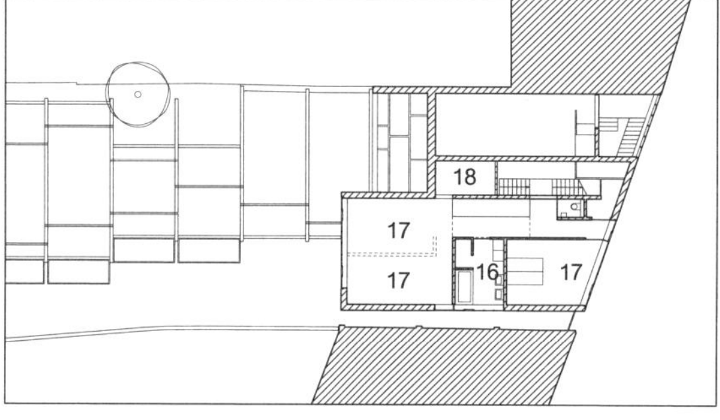

first floor plan

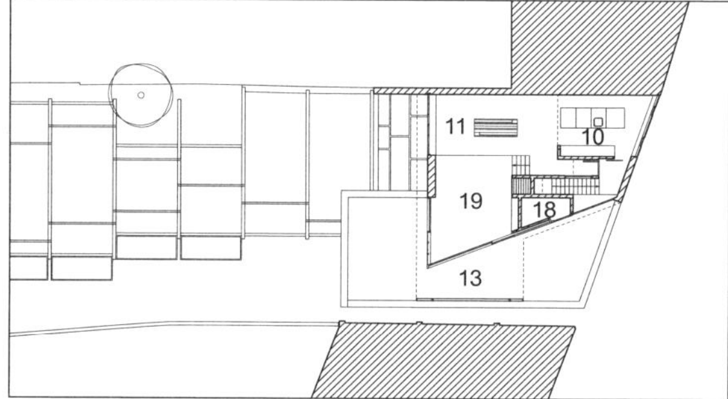

second floor plan

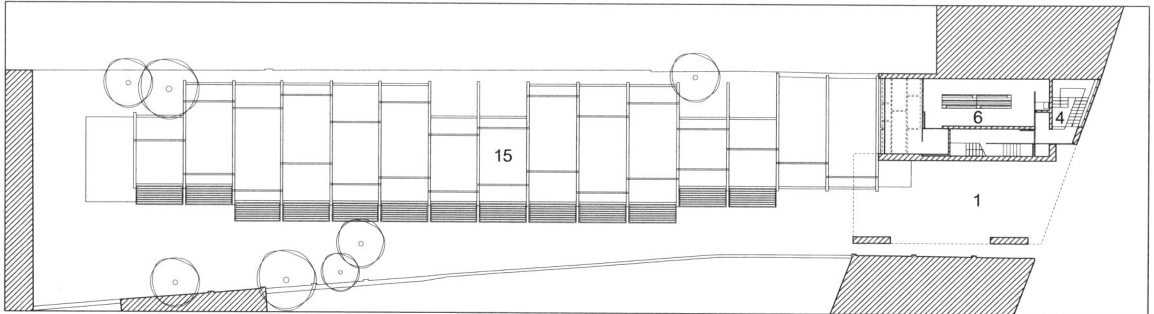

intermediate floor plan

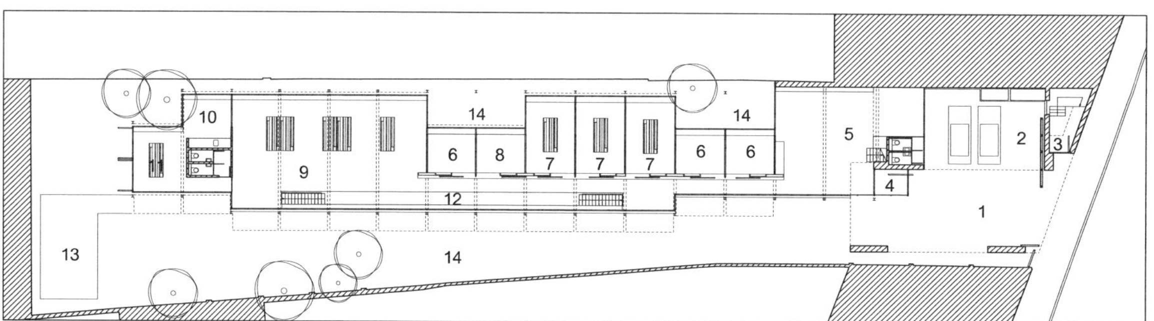

ground floor plan

MCMXCVI – 02
Refurbishment of the inner city central squares Korenmarkt, Emile Braunplein and Market Hall, Ghent, 1996-2012

Following two demolition campaigns carried out for a World Exhibition in 1913 and a never built administrative centre in the 1960s, the historic heart of Ghent had for decades deteriorated into a desolate carpark, languishing between three gothic towers. In two consecutive competitions between 1996 and 2005, Marie-José Van Hee architecten together with Robbrecht en Daem architecten proposed a new programme for the site, one that did not strictly adhere to the original competition brief. Rather than merely providing an open space for events, they sought to fill this void and reinstate the presence of previously existing civic spaces that had become unrecognisable over time, through the careful positioning of a new building, a Market Hall.

This new volume positions itself between Poeljemarkt, Goudenleeuwplein and a new lower-lying 'green' that adjoins the brasserie, bicycle parking, and public toilets below the hall. While the building occupies an obvious position on the 24,000 m² site, it has been carefully stitched into the urban fabric. Respecting the neighbouring towers of the Belfry and Sint-Niklaaskerk, the Market Hall instead takes its height from a lower group of buildings, among them the adjacent city hall, the building from which it also derives its profile.

As an urban interior, the inside envelops the passer-by under a dual modulated wooden ceiling, whose small windows scatter light inwards. The contemporary steel structure clad in wood and glass discretely distinguishes itself, by way of its form and finishing materials, from the historic stone buildings between which it unobtrusively assumes its place. A glazed envelope protects the wood, while at the same time lending a gentle sheen and softening the outline of the building. Overlapping glass tiles create a transparent edge where the ridge of the roof touches the sky, simultaneously diffusing and reflecting it.

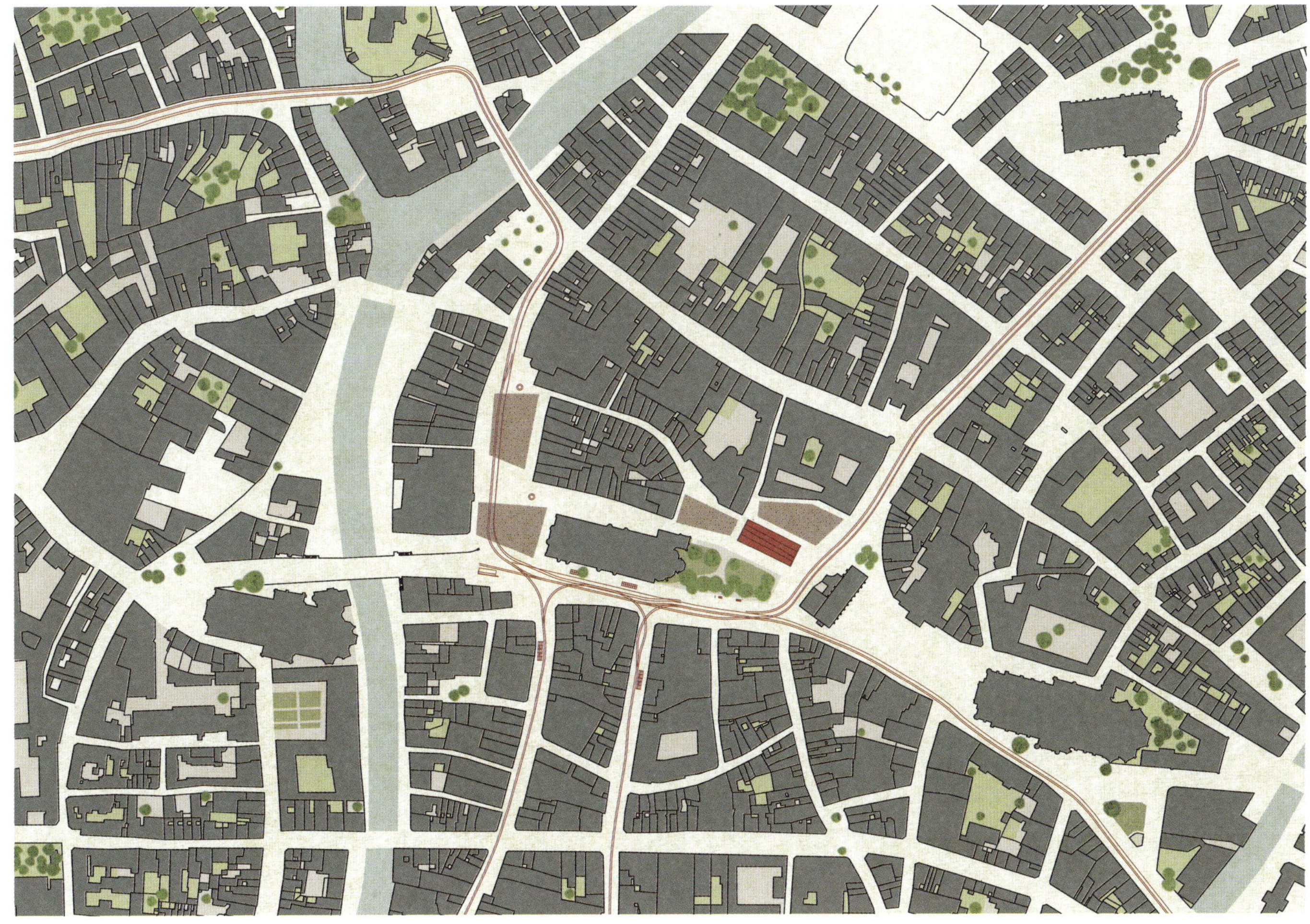

1/5000

The site is surrounded by a dozen protected monuments, including Sint-Niklaaskerk (13th century), the city hall (15th-17th century), the Belfry (15th century) and its *Mammelokker* (18th century), all registered as UNESCO World Heritage Sites since 1999.

The public realm was designed as a single entity within and in relation to the historic core of the city, although it was executed in different phases. The area covered by the project was originally conceived as a series of alternating green and paved urban spaces, but was not completed entirely according to plan. Korenmarkt was envisaged as a paved square, a free space where events could be held. The green takes over the greater part of Braunplein, with its fourteen carefully selected trees which will eventually grow into fully mature city trees. Sloping grass lawns planted with spring flowers form sunbathing spots which connect the street level with the lower-lying public facilities under the Market Hall. George Minne's statue group *De Fontein der Geknielden* (Fountain with Kneeling Youths) has been integrated into the park. Walls, benches and stairs in dark natural stone enclose the green spaces and the choir of Sint-Niklaaskerk, while light-coloured modular stone elements lie interlocked in sequence, like prehistoric vertebrae, to form low, curving walls that border the grassed areas and invite people to sit.

The squares and streets have been laid out without any changes in level, reinforcing the idea of a continuous urban space, with the pavement stretching unbroken between the façades of the street and the square. Together with various facilities for disabled people, the city centre has been made fully accessible to all. Thoughtfully designed street furniture – benches, public transport stops, bicycle parking, etc. – provides the visitor with easily recognisable places in the urban environment.

Large buffer basins for the harvesting of rainwater, the use of natural materials, the integration of public transport, and a clear vision for the re-evaluation of the historic centre and its old spatial structures represent forward-thinking answers to contemporary demands of sustainability.

Such concerns always form part of the thought process and the design attitude of the architects, supporting their ambition to make the centre of the city a social space where people can once again gather, meet, share and enjoy.

The project was finalist in the European Union Prize for Contemporary Architecture – Mies van der Rohe 2013.

ground floor plan

0   10   20   30 m

c. 1895

c. 1915

1996

A House on Pig Street

Marie-José Van Hee pursues architecture as an autonomous and authentic practice in an age where these qualities have diminished.

Photography has always struggled with authenticity. In its nascent stages, this was due to mechanical reproduction – it was reproducible. Now as images are created and distributed through digital means, there has been an extreme inflation in this condition.

To counter this, I attempt to make photographs that are unapologetically laconic and characterised by the descriptive rigour afforded by analogue means (film) and the denial (and simultaneously the assertion) of artistic will.

The house (the architect's own) depicted in the two photographs is built from simple stuff (brickwork, some concrete, timber, limestone, plaster, paint) but there is a measured complexity in the building's spatial constitution and its material articulation.

In this photograph, taken at night in the summer of 2008, the outer walls of the house, smeared with 'bastard' mortar, are partially illuminated by light from a house situated across the narrow medieval street in which it sits.

A House on Pig Street XXVII 2008

Five vertically attenuated windows sit at the outer face of the wall, each window divided into three vertically emphatic panes by two slender mullions.

In the photograph, there is significant recession in the size of the windows from left to right due to the oblique nature of the view, necessitated by the intimate quality of the street.

The intimacy of the interior with the street is enhanced by the rhythmic array of joists spanning the living room that can be seen through two of the windows from this viewpoint.

We often talk of the street entering the house, but not so often of how the interior can enter the street without compromising privacy.

The rhythm of the joists is echoed in the arrangement of lead seams on the underside of the gently projecting canopy above.

The building appears quite grand, almost stately. This is due not to the architecture, but to a slight exaggeration of scale (determined by the nature of the lens used) and the slightly contrived nature of the photograph's composition (determined by the viewpoint and frame chosen).

There are allusions in the architecture to permanence, but nothing lasts forever. It will though, one day, make the most beautiful of ruins.

A House on Pig Street XVI 2008

The space depicted, a fragment of the living room, is illuminated by soft daylight from the clerestory windows on the northeastern edge of the room.

It is a hinge between two wings.

It appears warm and familiar yet detached and ironic, like Gerhard Richter's painting of his then wife Ema descending a stair ("Ema (Nude on a Staircase)", 1966).

The stair is a vertical threshold connected to two other horizontal thresholds and a further vertical threshold. There is a conflation of space, a special architectural quality.

The opening on the ground floor leads, to the left, to the hallway of the most used entrance to the house and, to the right, down two steps, to the kitchen and bathroom.

The opening at the top of the stair leads, to the left, to a further stair behind the wall that connects with guest rooms above and, to the right, to Marie-José's library and bedroom.

A refrigerator sits in the space under the stair.

The stair is a rebellious act against prevailing conditions. Foregoing its restraining elements (balustrade and handrail – Luis Barragán insisted they were only required by the infirm), it resembles a stair that descends into a garden.

This perception is reinforced by the lime stone floor on which the stair lands. A solid block of the material is used to bring two conditions together.

The stair is constructed of brickwork spanned with concrete lintels, dressed with limestone on the treads and risers and plaster and paint on the wall that supports it. The stone is mitred to make a seamless edge. One can imagine the pleasure of applying plaster from a trowel against stone to achieve such an exacting joint.

There are marks on the painted walls where hands have been applied to steady the body ascending or descending the stair.

The stair has been used in many ways. My twin children (as four year olds) exploited its spatial condition and learnt to jump from height, one step at a time.

The stair is a touchstone for the house. It navigates a space between pleasure and austerity, like life itself should.

House Van Hee, 1994

Le Puy-Notre-Dame, 2008-2022

A Family House

After the untimely death of their parents, the Van Hee children wanted to maintain a tangible bond. A shared place that they could go to, to celebrate being together. A country house. Italy would be ideal. Only unreasonably far away. Just within reach was the Loire Valley. Marie-José has a long-standing affinity with the region. Not so much for the river. The hilly, varied landscape, the colour of the limestone, the weathered opulence, the culture of the vineyards. She has often gone for long hikes there in the past.

It had to be a house in a village. With a history, and definitely not renovated. There was work to be done, a lot of work. Marie-José had to have the time, the space and the freedom to sculpt the building as she saw fit. With evident respect to draw windows and doors where she felt they should be.

After a long search, initially through estate agents who did not understand what the Van Hees wanted, they finally had success with a notary. In the centre of Le Puy-Notre-Dame, in the shadow of the village church with its defining pinnacles. From afar, high atop its hill, the village – which was once a prosperous town – dominates the surrounding area. A silhouette that beckons to Umbria and Tuscany.

The house itself was not interesting. What appealed to Marie-José were the outbuildings. A sixteenth-century noble canon's house, whose most recent owner was a winegrower.

Le Puy-Notre-Dame, 2008-2022

116

The inner courtyard with a gatehouse, full of clutter, entirely built up with outhouses added over hundreds of years. The interior disfigured beyond recognition, brutally carved up by partitions and internal walls. Already making plans, it was discovered that the closed sewing shop of the neighbour was an integral part of the original demesne. The cottage was bought, and the property once again lay between two streets. Being able to leave through both the front and the back gives a sense of freedom. Marie-José's house in Ghent has the same means of escape.

More than eight years have now passed. In between there has been a lot of hard work. With French and Belgian contractors. Family and friends. The house has regained its nobility and former splendour. Large rooms with monumental fireplaces, the spiral staircase worn through centuries of use. An ingenious terrace with a contemporary glass addition. New timeless, sensuous bathrooms. Light, above all, light. As only true masters can accomplish. The signature of the master builder. Everything still empty, waiting for the inhabitants who want to forget the dust left behind by the builders. When I come to photograph the house, a friend has travelled there with Marie-José. He is full of admiration. In love with the place he saw take shape over the years. He calls the house the architect's child. It will never be finished. Just as children will continue to grow.

Le Puy-Notre-Dame, 2008-2022

Le Puy-Notre-Dame, 2008-2022

119

About Venice, 2018

*Marie-José gives space to life itself. She makes place with
walls, body and spirit come home.*

*Much like her struggle, if Hesse's 'Narziss und Goldmund'
was a building and not a book, she would be the author.*

The story of a pious heretic, or a frivolous nun.

*José builds monastic and spatial, robust and fragile, strict
and playful, old and new.*

No laughter without tears, no tears without laughter.

*She invites the senses into a room for the soul, a space where
the tops of your wings can never touch the walls.
Eternally empty, always just for someone.*

*José is a cat, she hisses at ugliness, purrs at beauty and
scratches what is false, and those who pet her.*

*Because she only wants to give, both now and thereafter.
As Palladio still gives, or Van Eyck. Generosity is the key to
Heaven, and Heaven is empty.*

Needless to say, we can do this together …

DIRK BRAECKMAN, M.J.-H.G.-18 #1

I have lived in this place since my student days. In those days it was still a small two room house, that I had renovated by myself. The whole street was owned by one man. I was interested in buying the house, since I had already carried out so many improvement works on it. At the beginning of the eighties the owner wanted to sell all the houses in the street, although not individually. Subsequently I ended up buying my house, along with the three neighbouring ones. At the time no-one was interested in living in this neighbourhood, next to Prinsenhof in Ghent: it was a working class area of dishevelled cottages inhabited by local people, who drank a lot and spoke in popular Ghent dialect. But they left you in peace, were always ready to help if it was needed, and it was customary to just leave your door unlocked.

I was in no hurry to rebuild. It took several years before the plans were ready to make a home out of it. And obtaining a building permit took a certain amount of persuasiveness – they were not entirely convinced, specifically with the height of the windows in the front façade. In order to defend my plans, I brought photographs of Ghent *bel étage* houses to the planning committee. I find it important that the windows here are the way they are: placed high and with narrow subdivisions. The house is open, towards the patio at the back, but at the same time closed, towards the façade at the front. I don't want people to be able to just look inside. Glass is for me just as much a barrier as a wall: it has a materiality, it is present. I pay a lot of attention to the detailing and the profile of windows, because this materiality fascinates me.

The rhythm in the façades of the adjacent houses was the inspiration for the elevation – the regularity

1/2500

and the spacing between windows, alternating with solid areas of wall. When building this house, the surroundings were taken into consideration. Architecture is bound to its context: the colour palettes of houses in Mexico, for example, would not be appropriate here, thus I have tried to integrate this house so that it corresponds as much as possible with the other houses. The total width of the façade is now 15 metres, but inside you still feel that there were once four houses: there are three staircases, two front doors, and the spaces are arranged in an L-form around a covered gallery and a patio. A large tree has always stood there, just as it did when I still lived in that one small house. Since you can't just get rid of a tree, I drew the plans around it.

No lawn has been laid out, and the toilet is still outside. Simply because I have no need for grass, and no need for luxury. I attach absolutely no importance to furniture.

A table, chairs and a bed, those you need, but I have no need for a lounge, thus there is none here. I like neutral spaces, with many possibilities. I want to make spaces with the correct proportions, and good light. I also like to work with level differences between different rooms: simplicity can thus acquire a certain complexity, and vice versa. As much as possible I choose natural and solid materials. The use of any material invariably references a specific time period: you can date a building on the basis of its material. By contrast, the space is something that can and must be timeless. Space is universal.

Marie-José Van Hee

The project was finalist in the European Union Prize for Contemporary Architecture – Mies van der Rohe in 1999.

1 entrance
2 kitchen
3 shower room
4 gallery
5 patio
6 library
7 bedroom
8 garden
9 garden storage
10 fireplace

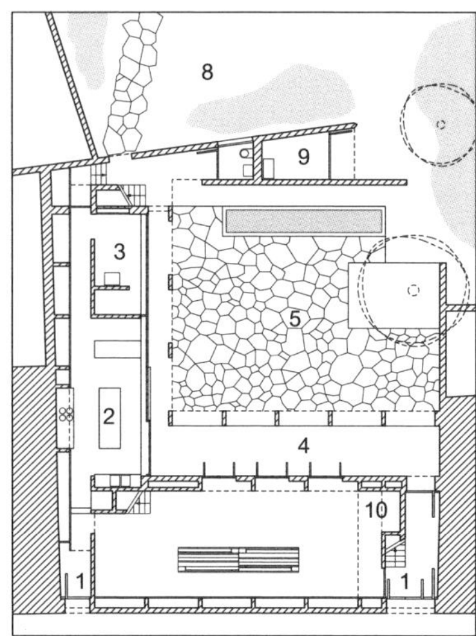

ground floor plan

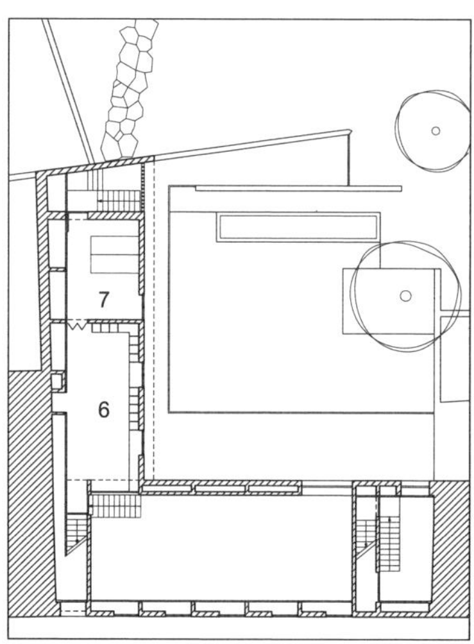

intermediate floor plan

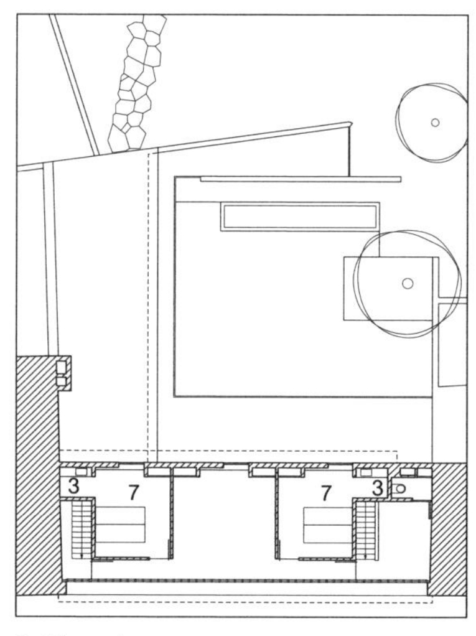

first floor plan

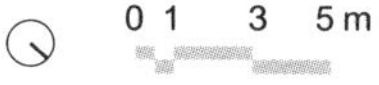

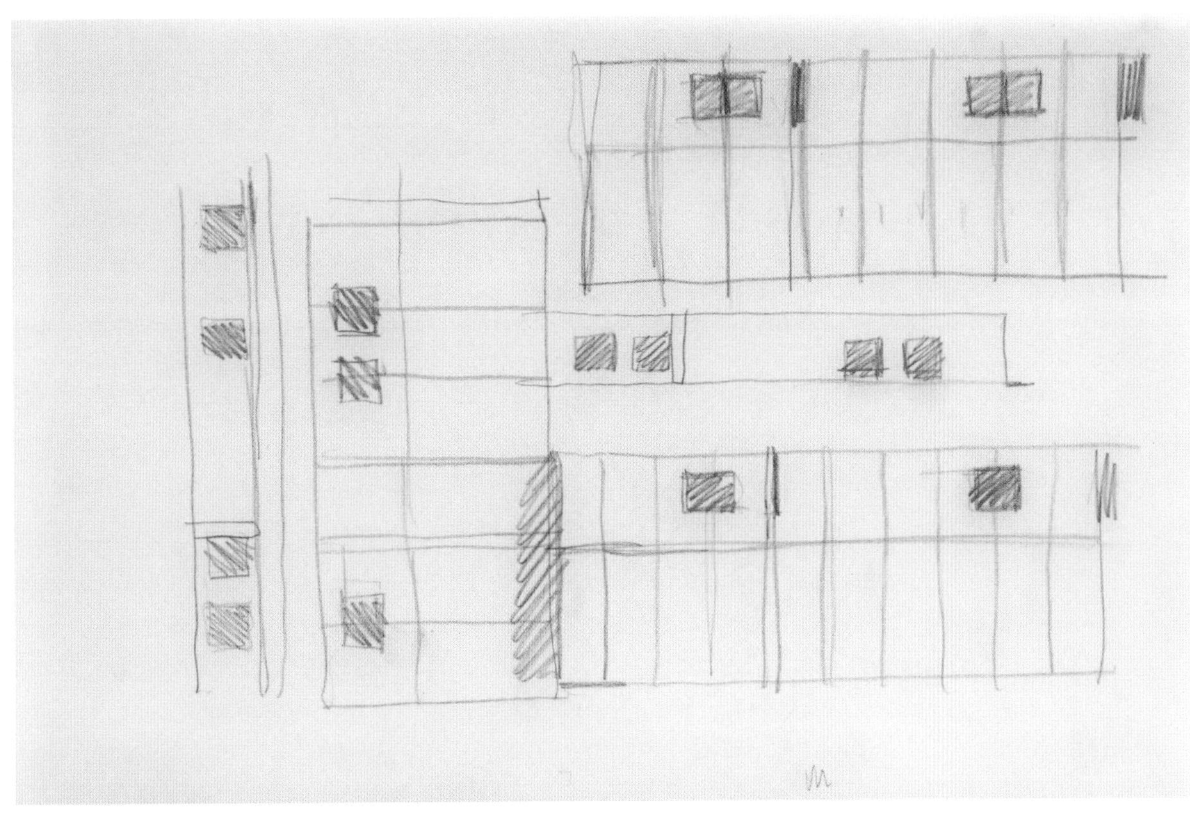

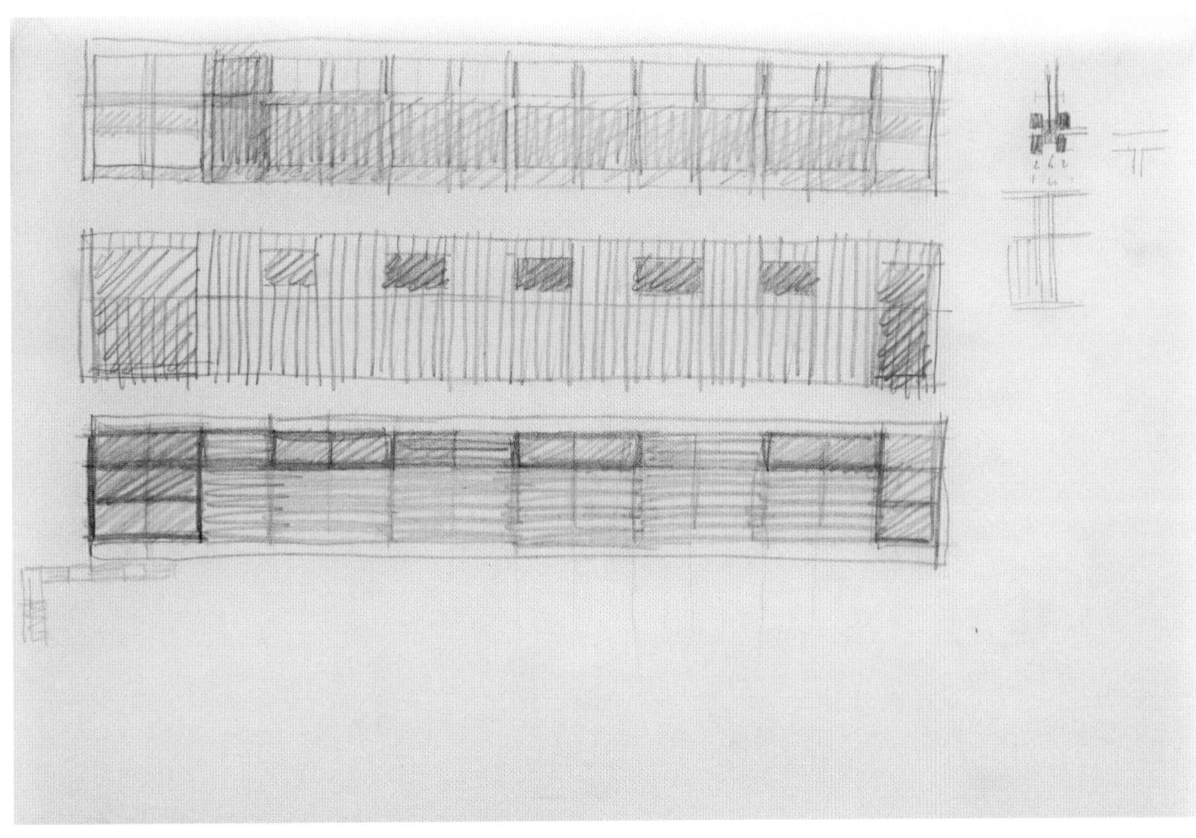

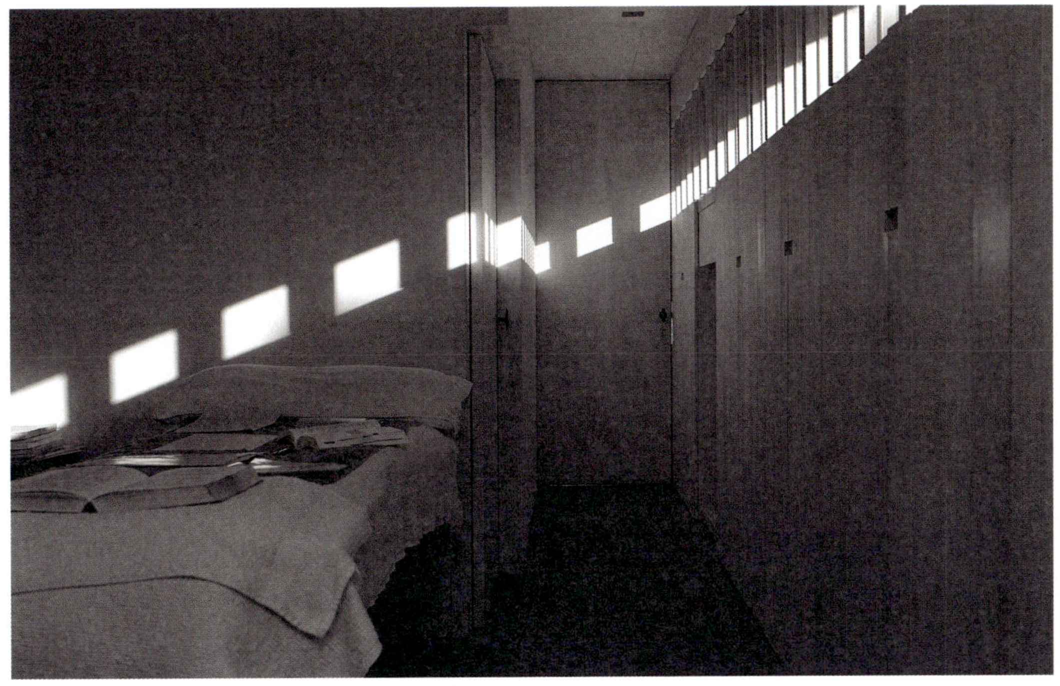

Cases and Ruins
(the furniture, interiors and architecture of Marie-José Van Hee)

Christian Kieckens

In 1993, the arts centre deSingel in Antwerp presented an exhibition dedicated to the work of Marie-José Van Hee. There was no specific title for the exhibition, and no personal introduction at the opening, apart from a small concert featuring a piece of music from Luigi Nono. In the foyer there were no drawings to be found on the wall, only four models, and eight lecterns, each with a book in which the work was printed.

The actual substance of her work, the built, is tacitly to be found in the reality of the world, not verbally reduced.[1]

Writing about Van Hee's oeuvre – in this case the furniture, fixed as well as freestanding – is contemplating this reality in which and in how every realisation, permanent or temporary, out of necessity or without obligation, is created, and why it exists as it does. The majority of her work is situated in the context of dwelling, and even in projects for the public realm it is concerned with 'nestling', 'feeling good' in oneself, defining and determining. It is an attempt to become aware of a 'hunger' for the essential, for the detail, for the subject matter, and for the care in the profession, the concern for 'making', and through that making to achieve more than merely that which is made. It refers therefore to mastery in the deepest sense of the word.

This essay is in the first place a *tribute* to the small scale in Van Hee's work, a eulogy for something most critics and writers tend to overlook. It subsequently expresses my personal appreciation for transcending the profession, and for a warmheartedness in life and work.

To build a house is to create a shelter against, and also within, nature and the (urban) landscape. In this respect it is about ruins, whether or not to fill in. What do these ruins mean in Van Hee's own oeuvre, for the locale in Flanders, and what does it mean for the profession? Each of these built ruins is the result of a long period of time between the first sketch and finally coming into use. The result reflects the process of increasingly complex mutual demands, and a sometimes incongruous overlap between the private and the public. But it is precisely in this 'overlap' that the significance of Van Hee's oeuvre lies hidden. It seems as if the projects are evident, as if they had come effortlessly into existence, as if they had always been there. Talking about her own house in Ghent she states, 'they think that my house is a renovation', which demonstrates that a house from her hand and mind nestles itself indistinguishably upon its site, becoming *genius loci*. At the same time the house also stands quietly, without shouting, unobtrusive, because it is a private building, not a monument. A house should not be conspicuous, which is not to say that it cannot make a place upon its site. And it is that 'made place' that manifests itself through a range of qualities such as the tangible precision in spatial planning; the choice, handling and the naturalness of materials; the artisanal realisation, and with it the accompanying concern for accuracy. No addition of colour, no superfluous material, only a manifestation of utmost mastery and control. Every rationale about 'how' and 'why' and 'by which' with regard to the representation of buildings designed by her is transcended by a thorough reflection on the formation of spatial sequences in the design of a personalised house. The result of this is that every design has a characteristic signature, related to her way of thinking, but transcending any form of localness.

To maintain, that is the essence of Van Hee's work: *maintenir, tenir en mains*, to hold onto. There is no better description for the understanding of the craft of building than the term 'tenacity'. These continually recurring principles manifest themselves in many of her houses, some of them visible, others more tangible. The first recurring example is the introduction of the patio in her projects. An outdoor room with enclosed courtyard that offers both views and light as well as a relationship with nature; internalised outdoor space, *hortus conclusus*. This enclosed garden does not stand alone, but forms part of a sequence of spaces that make secondary outdoor circulation routes possible, punctuated by programmatic transitions. In this way each of the outdoor spaces stands apart, and the interval spaces – primarily for storage – become a *poché*. Another functional principle is the development of the interior in such a way that the walls are formed with and by cupboards. In analogy to historic buildings, the walls in her work possess a thickness, protecting against every manner of intrusion. Cupboard walls are thus the solution to safeguard the interior against every possible form of unwanted and uncontrolled discomfort. These thick walls consequently structure the interior, but furthermore, they are the infrastructure that ensures no more freestanding furniture needs to be added. Furniture is a temporary addition; a building usually exists for a longer period of time.

According to Van Hee, 'a building must be finished once the structure is completed'. This is for her an incentive to design all of her projects in such a way that later constructive or architectural additions are unnecessary, that is to say: the essence lies in the structure. She is annoyed by the mandatory use of moisture-repellent membranes and prescribed thicknesses for insulation and the like. 'This sort of thing does not help us build a better building', she adds. The building for the communications agency Bailleul in Ghent also originated from this notion, along with a programme of office and dwelling – working and living as the most essential functions – which over the course of time can undergo changes in use. Building is a lengthy process, of accepting and rejecting, of fighting for a conviction. Building is an answer to long term and adaptable use.

Van Hee takes the profession *au sérieux*. Everything is considered, nowhere is anything left to chance – except in the search itself where chance forms an approach, and as a result another solution is created.

In her work the notion of 'context' has a specific place: the locale of the place where it is to be built, as much as the reading of the site. The craftsman who takes pride in his work, the engineer who determines the breaking point between fragility and steadfastness, clients who with their faith and confidence in the architect provide the required space, the project architects who with their 'hunger' guide each process; all make up the framework within which the work is created and made. Making is the most important thing that happens in and with the work: every project is made.

Setting foot inside a house by Van Hee is always another sensation; one comes to a higher awareness of experiencing the transition from outside to inside. One feels oneself welcomed in the enclosed space, the true meaning of *entrata*, and is taken by a particular everyday-ness *a particolarità*.

A house is for the client, for private use and personal enjoyment. Every house has non-transferable and therefore inherent robust details that were not conceived for the sake of aesthetics or 'the demonstration of expertise', but from a sense of how to build as correctly as possible.

But what now with regard to making a ruin liveable? From where and when does the second layer of interventions arise? Ruins have niches, or were designed with niches to make the stringency of architecture more appropriate to life, to add a use to it. Living is a verb, a form of use, and this living takes place in every house and not merely in a home. More than 300 types of 'houses' can be defined using German grammatical characters, something that our Dutch, also a Germanic language, has lost through its closer proximity to the Anglo-Saxon world. The German word *Haus*, originating from the concept of *huan*, covers much more than just the idea of 'home'. In the English language it became *house*. *Krankenhaus* becomes in Dutch *hospitaal* (hospital), *Schulhaus* becomes *school* (school), *Hochhaus* is *torengebouw* (towerblock), *Mehrfamilienhaus* is *wooncomplex* (housing complex). Will the multilayeredness of language thus increasingly continue to be lost? And is a *Haus* in the original sense nothing but a built ruin with thresholds between outside and inside, with alcoves and niches, a place of protection?

And are there not small and large spaces therein, where furniture – fixed as well as freestanding – is placed and consequently defines the use? And is it not so that the furniture then offers its own *raison d'être* that is independent from the architecture, and likewise independent from the profession of architecture? And do we then speak of another trade or mastery? Furniture, which is replaceable but sufficiently resistant to the whims of every zeitgeist. All arguments speak about the craftsman in both design and execution.

Around ninety years ago, Adolf Loos wrote on the theme of furniture: his appreciation for the craftsman and the question of whether every new style was appropriate. In his short essay *Und noch einmal zum Thema: 'Der Stuhl'* from 1929 he cites the following: 'Und da komme ich zur wichtigsten Frage der neuen Formgebung: alle Ansichten, die jetzt überall dahin gehen, dass das Sitzmöbel von unseren Körpermassen abhängig ist, sind falsch. Es ist überall der gleiche Körper, dem die Sitzmöbel dienen sollen und wie verschieden sind durch die Jahrtausende die Formen! Was ein Sesselmuseum oder Stuhlmuseum zeigen sollte. Wer diese Lehre nich begreift, sollte die Hand davon lassen. Das hat meine Vortragsreihe: "Der Mensch mit dem modernen Nerven" für alle Gebrauchsgegenstände lehren wollte.'[2]

A second text from Adolf Loos from the same year, *Möbel und Menschen – Zu einem Handwerksbuch* gives yet another clarification. Loos writes: 'Ich bin glücklich, dieses Buch (*Abraham und David Roentgen und ihre Neuwieder Möbelwerkstatt*) in Handen zu halten. David Roentgen ist immer als idol neben meinem leben hergegangen, obwohl ich nicht mehr von ihm wusste, als dass er gelebt und der grossen Katharina einen schreibtisch für zwanzigtausend taler verkauft hatte, den sie so exorbitant billig fand, das sie den kaufpreis erhöhte. Wohl niemand hat diese geschichte so häufig und mit solchem nachdruck erzählt wie ich; denn ich bin davon überzeugt, dass sich das handwerk durch solche anerkennung zur vollsten blüte entfaltet. Aber die Katharinen scheinen ausgestorben zu sein'.[3]

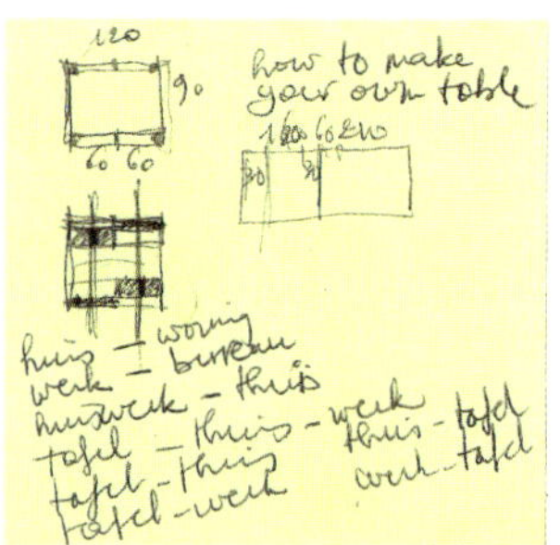

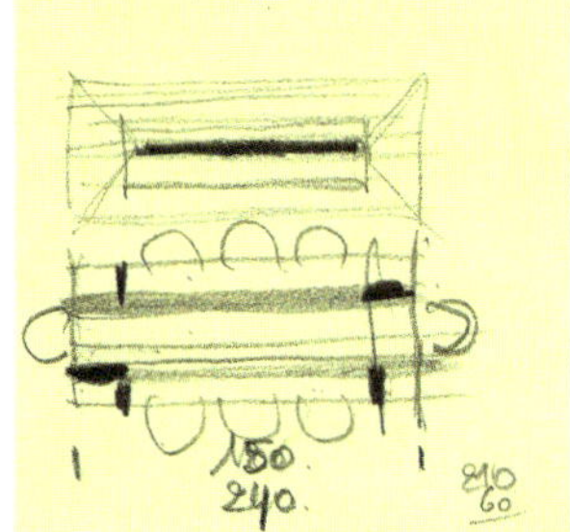

huis-werk-tafel, 2011–2017

Besides seated furniture such as chairs and sofas which were made by Joseph Veillich and referenced other furniture (for instance by Thomas Chipperfield) but adapted to specific guidelines, Loos also designed small pieces of furniture that can be labelled miniature architecture. These included side tables with an excessive amount of 'columns', nightstands and chest of drawers in which an obvious architectonic structure or lining is present, and which were sometimes integrated into wooden panelling. The fact that Loos considered the relationship with architecture to be evident is perhaps most visible in his glass champagne cooler. The round bottle cooler is lined with hollowed-out fragments in the shape of an ionic column, with the accompanying glasses remaining cool when placed therein.

1   LA MAISON DE LA CAVE AU GRENIER LE SENS DE LA HUTTE
Car la maison est notre coin du monde. Elle est – on l'a souvent dit – notre premier univers.[4]
[24]

Placing the furniture by Marie-José Van Hee via these philosophical phrases from Norberg-Schulz, and with Loos as a historical reflection, is essential in any overview of her work because it offers an insight into her thought process. Van Hee herself says, 'Designing a piece of furniture as such doesn't interest me. If someone calls me up for a cupboard or the like, I am not particularly interested. Except when I see in situ that the problem isn't a cupboard, but a space that is not functioning well. Then it comes down to making an essential alteration in the architectonic relationship, so I see it as a challenge to do something with the space.'

2   MAISON ET UNIVERS
Etrange situation, les espaces qu'on aime ne veulent pas toujours être enfermés! Ils se déploient.
[63]

Need, want and necessity, these are thus the three concepts applicable in the development of the interior spaces in Van Hee's projects. There is a need for storing things away, for a place to prepare food, for cladding the ruins of the house. 'Architecture protects furniture and furniture protects things which are found at the core of the core. In this way, people can experience their surroundings as meaningful. Since meaning implies that small things can be understood as condensations of the wider world, and that the world is explained through things.'[5]

3   TIROIR, COFFRES ET ARMOIRES
L'espace intérieur à l'armoire est un espace d'intimité, un espace qui ne s'ouvre pas à tout venant.
[83]

It is clear that the following two manifestations of furniture can be noted: the integrated and the freestanding. The first is fixed and contained within the ruins of architecture, the second can be placed and relocated according to one's needs, giving expression to the experience of the occupant. Furthermore, it is equally evident that an architect designs furniture in a different manner than an industrial designer. An architect reasons from structure and infilling, from uniqueness/particularity, an industrial designer from maximal useability and production of the object. In his introductory essay *Pieter*

De Bruyne en de betekenis van het meubel, Christian Norberg-Schulz, alongside all other critical reflections on furniture, outlines it as follows: 'Only when the interior is furnished does it become a place', 'As *imago mundi* it brings together the interior and exterior world', and 'concealing and revealing' are in fact part of the structure of memory. Bachelard says accordingly: 'Cases are objects that can be *opened*.'[6]

4   LE NID
La maison-nid n'est jamais jeune. On pourrait dire, sur un mode pédant, qu'elle est le lieu naturel de la fonction d'habiter.
[99]

What do these intentions say then, that there is a constant need for expression of being, or of being oneself? Being oneself, from an absence, an emptiness, something that was not yet there. It is the same for Van Hee: 'The motivation behind her furniture designs is usually a personal need. Around twenty years ago, Van Hee designed beds for her own house, with futons that were raised off the ground. A simple structure: an oak frame, painted white, with cedar planks on which the futon could lie. This piece of furniture started to lead a life of its own, and in 2016 was adapted to create the present bed-bank with its multiple uses. The oak frame was revised and divided into two longitudinal elements. The structure of the bed consists on the one longitudinal side of two legs on the corners connected by a beam, and on the other side an identical beam with two recessed legs.'[7]

5   LA COQUILLE
La meilleure marque de l'émerveillement c'est l'exagération.
[107]

The textile walls for *Sanft und Seide* by Lily Reich; the concrete structure as an enlarged table for Flora Ruchat's own house; lying in the grass against a tree, legs aloft, inspired the *chaise-longue* from Charlotte Perriand; Petra Blaisse's moving curtain walls and her mobilisation of space; the occupation of the stage in the scenography of Pina Bausch; the use of furniture as plinths and frames for the placing of bodies in the sculptures of Berlinde De Bruyckere; and the design of oversized ruins by Grafton Architects … the range is extensive, but not endless. Women who as *grand dames* in the world of design ignore the purely formal, who incorporate furniture and architecture in their own work. Similarly, Marie-José Van Hee: nothing superfluous, but meaningful presence. Structure, nothing else.

6   LES COINS
Mais d'abord, le coin est un refuge qui nous assure une première valeur de l'être : l'immobilité.
[131]

Buildings appear expressive, whereas furniture seems stringently contained within the domestic ruins. The house is in a certain sense similarly designed, from a demand of the client and with a series of organisational adjustments. In every case there is a highly existential space to be found in this transition zone between the high and low volume, between inside and outside, between the front and back, between the ground floor and the roof space. These are almost undefined gradations that a client hardly stipulates, but for Van Hee they are precisely what form a sequential junction in the circulatory route and diagram of the dwelling: a space that is unprejudiced, that can be finished to one's satisfaction, as a result perfectly user-friendly.

7 LA MINIATURE

Comme les grandes valeurs d'être et de non-être sont diffi-
ciles à situer! Le silence, où est sa racine, est-il une gloire du
non-être ou une domination de l'être? Il est 'profond'. Mais où
est la racine de sa profondeur?
[165]

Marie-José Van Hee has not (as yet) designed a lot of freestanding
furniture: a table, a bed, a case. But that also says a lot: what is more
essential in life than sitting/working/talking at a table, sleeping in
a bed, and storing things away in a case or cupboard? Every time
she knows exactly how to formulate simple and direct solutions: the
rotation of the legs of the table in order to create a different image.
Recently she developed an edition of the huis-werk-tafel (house-
work-table) with wooden legs that took the place of the original
metal ones. Other principles too repeatedly recur: the application
of vertical supports under a frame, or even the division of content
and casing; a leather compartment within a wooden structure, with
a serving tray on top. The only frivolity which Van Hee permits herself is the colour of the wood, in different colours of white, green and
blue …

8 L'IMMENSITÉ INTIME

L'immensité est en nous. … Dès que nous sommes immobiles,
nous sommes ailleurs; nous rêvons dans un monde immense.
[169]

Could it be said that the current pattern whereby a thing becomes *a
priori* art, is not applicable in this case? To be of service and thereby
facilitate a use, is not the same as to create something functional
or elevate something to the level of art. Katrien Vandermarliere
writes: 'Marie-José Van Hee does not consider furniture to be art
or design, yet her furniture designs are based on a certain ambiguity. This can already be seen in the names given to each piece. Bed-
bank (bed-bench) can be used either as a bed or as a bench. Huis-
werk-tafel (house-work-table) is a worktable that can stand in the
kitchen, patio, gallery or garden. The twin uses for each piece of furniture are also a manner whereby the number of objects is limited in
favour of '*Lebensraum*' or living space.'[8]

9 DIALECTIQUE DU DEDANS ET DU DEHORS

La chambre est, en profondeur, notre chambre. La chambre est
en nous. Nous ne la voyons plus. Elle ne nous limite plus, car
nous sommes au fond même de son repos, dans le repos qu'elle
nous a conféré? Et toutes les chambres de jadis viennent s'em-
boîter dans cette chambre-ci. Comme tout est simple!
[203]

Is the architectonic thinking of Van Hee only concerned with furniture in the common meaning of the word: objects which one can
sit on, lie on, store things in; or is it about more than that? Does it go
beyond the image of furniture? A panelling, an encasing, a *poché* that
leaves the useable space free from every form of spatial interpretation, and therefore creates no strain? What about staircases as furniture, what about kitchens, or bathrooms? 'In her designs for houses,
the furniture is an integral part of the space: rooms and circulation
areas. Walls, staircases, galleries and so on become concealed cupboards, cloakrooms, workspaces, alcoves or bookcases. Tables, chairs
and beds are for Van Hee the only moveable furniture that belongs
in a house. The freestanding pieces of furniture contribute to the

top: Reconversion House Devos, 1999-2002
middle left: House HdF, 2007-2011 / middle right: Reconversion House Verstraete – Compernolle, 2007-2012
bottom: Refurbishment Riverbanks Leie, 2009 – ongoing

changes of use, and can be recycled or passed down. They are added and moved by the occupants for various purposes and in different seasons and stages of life, and can be moved out again. They will not make any fundamental changes to the space or the effect of light.'[9]

10   LA PHENOMENOLOGIE DU ROND
Ainsi, sans commentaire, Van Gogh a écrit: « La vie est probablement ronde. » Et Joë Bousquet, sans avoir connu la phrase de Van Gogh, écrit: « On lui a dit que la vie est belle. Non! La vie est ronde »[10]
[208]

Buildings were conceived and made in order to 'house'. The interior of a house in this sense belongs intrinsically to the building, but at the same time it possesses its own expression. Van Hee creates habitable living spaces, she makes a personal habit, *un habit personnel, une habitation personnalisée* (a personal dress/habit, a custom home). Converting this habit to reality as precisely as possible happens through a mastery in which she knows how to maintain control, in spite of all the opposition and resistance and the accompanying mental battle. The beginning and preservation of each project is undeniably rooted in a reality of adaptation and acceptance, and a form of resistance or tenacity. An interaction between the temporary and the permanent.

Notes

1   Since 1985 the deSingel arts centre in Antwerp has hosted exhibitions showcasing Belgian and international architecture, with curators including Carolina De Backer, Katrien Vandermarliere and Moritz Küng. This was initiated in Ghent in 1983 by the Foundation for Architecture in Flanders (Stichting voor Architectuur/SAM) with Christian Kieckens and Marc Dubois.

2   And now I get to the most important question of the new design: all opinions that now universally tend to say that a seat depends on our body mass, are false. It is everywhere the same body that seats should serve, and how different the forms are through the millennia! This is what a sofa museum or a chair museum should show. Anyone who does not understand this teaching should leave it alone. This is what my lecture series "Man with the Modern Nerve" wanted to teach for all everyday objects.' Adolf Opel (ed.), *Adolf Loos – Gesammelte Schriften* (Wien: Lesethek Verlag, 2010) pp. 705-706.

3   'I am happy to hold this book (Abraham und David Roentgen und ihre Neuwieder Möbelwerkstatt) in my hands. David Roentgen has always acted as an idol during my life, although I did not know more about him than that he had lived and sold the great Katharina a writing table for twenty thousand thaler, which she found so exorbitantly cheap, that she increased the purchase price. Surely no one has told this story as often and as emphatically as I have, for I am convinced that through such acknowledgement, craftsmanship will flourish to its fullest. But the Katharinas seem to have become extinct.' Adolf Loos, *Trotzdem* (Innsbruck: Brenner Verlag, 1931) p. 242.

4   Gaston Bachelard, *La poétique de l'espace* (Paris: Presses Universitaires de France, 1957).

5   Christian Norberg-Schulz, Jos Vanderperren, *Pieter De Bruyne, 25 jaar meubels*, (Gent: Stad Gent, 1980) p. 12.

6   Ibid., p. 11.

7   Katrien Vandermarliere, MANIERA 16 press release, 'Noble and Adaptable. The furniture of Marie-José Van Hee', 2017, on the occasion of an exhibition of furniture by Marie-José Van Hee and textiles by Marie Mees and Cathérine Biasino in Galerie MANIERA, Brussels, 30.11.2017-28.02.2018.

8   Ibid.

9   Ibid.

10 Joë Bousquet, *Le meneur de lune*, 1946, p. 174.

The first section in this text contains amended excerpts from 'Habitus en weerbarstigheid' by Christian Kieckens, published in *Architectural Review Flanders*, No. 10, (Antwerp: Flemish Architecture Institute, 2012), edited by Christoph Grafe. Gaston Bachelard's book *La poétique de l'espace* is taken as a reference for the second part of the text. The numbers refer to the relevant pages of the text extracts, taken from the fourth edition published by Quadrige in 1989.

House Leroux, 2010-2015

The garden room
Geert Leroux in conversation with
Katrien Vandermarliere

Since 1986 we have lived in a house with a doctor's surgery designed by the architect Paul Felix. Over the years, the original building has been converted to meet the needs of the family. There were meticulous changes to the interior by Jean-Claude Lerouge and a garden design with water feature by the landscape architect Paul De Roose. For a troublesome extension to the back of the original house that turned out to have inadequate foundations, we were once again obliged to call in an architect. But again, being aware that we live in a piece of 'heritage', we wanted to engage a skilful and inspired architect. Through Chantal's research and serious interest, and above all through conversations with the textile designer Marie Mees, we came into contact with Marie-José Van Hee. Our request was a purely constructional problem – a subsiding extension and what to do with it. The use to which a new rear extension would be put was developed in conversation with Marie-José Van Hee. It was to be a garden room that connected with my workroom via a broad doorway. A handsome, spacious, square room with two glass walls facing the garden. Next to it is a room temporarily used for storage, but which is prepared for future use as a bathroom. As a result, the ground floor could later be used as accommodation for the elderly. That is Marie-José Van Hee's strength. You think of an extra storeroom with a cubby-hole to work in and what you get is architecture!

House Leroux, 2010-2015

The original interior of the doctor's surgery designed by Paul Felix – which is now my workroom – is still intact and the passage to the garden room is clad in walnut veneer in the same 'study style'. The garden room, with a ceiling in concrete cast onsite in wooden formwork, is a potent space. Irregularly-arranged floor slabs in shell-bearing limestone run on from the garden room to the patio.

The original outside staircase, which ran from the terrace on the first floor in a straight line towards the garden, was removed. A new transverse staircase in solid blocks of stone between two concrete walls leads into the garden in a different way, in a curve, and adds privacy to the ground floor patio. This gives rise to a completely different relationship between the house and the garden, on both floors.

This is also facilitated by the simple steel structure designed by engineer Dirk Jaspaert, a slender pergola across the full width of the south front. In addition, the strategically positioned flower tubs on the patio provide shade and intimacy. Climbers including wisteria and Ebbinge's silverberry add the natural and fanciful element to this coherent composition.

In this way, the building became a process with surprising results that we, the clients, would never have expected. A constructional problem led to a dialogue about demolition, rebuilding, new living spaces and the garden. But how do you retain the character of the 1962 house and how does the architect manoeuvre within these boundaries? It was astonishing to see how Marie-José Van Hee, an architect who very clearly has her own style, has added to Paul Felix's modernist architecture and Jean-Claude Lerouge's later adaptations without affronting them. It was actually with great pleasure

that we evolved in parallel with her proposals in the course of this dialogue. As a result of her intervention, we have come to understand that even though we have lived here for thirty years, we can still live in a different way in this house. Marie-José Van Hee's insight, making the relationship with the garden more intense, connecting the garden and our experience of it to the house, is something we find very rewarding. She resolved this division between the house and the garden for us, not only with architecture, but also by means of such a simple change as the removal of part of the beech hedge that traverses the garden. The result of all this is that we have also started to live differently; having breakfast on the patio, and living in the garden room on summery days or behind the glass in winter.

House HdF, 2007-2011

Youkali

The milestone of fifty years is coming up and you resolve no longer to live out of your suitcase, but rather to finally find a place you want to call 'home'. But where will I do it? In the bustle of the city or more withdrawn, but just close enough to a range of possibilities? Fell for a property with old trees, a decrepit house from the end of the 1800s, an old barn and two ponds. But above all close to sea and beach. And believe me, that means a special sort of light. In your mind too.

And then the grand manoeuvres start. Because actually you have too much 'Sturm und Drang' and want to get started as quickly as possible. But on what? You don't really know, so you look for a direction and guidance and find them; after a thrilling audience *in Ghent I was able to go on to the next round.*

And then the time and reflection came naturally: what do you actually want and when do you want it to be ready? The 'what' turned into an engrossing exercise in which I was challenged to make choices and then revise them again. Speaking with some caution, I can say that the asker of the questions also had changes of opinion and insight, but no matter, as the motive was always to make it better. It was assumed that you also understood and agreed. Or else she said it wasn't yet pure enough. Now I know what that means.

I was once given a book on 'Wabi Sabi'. Fortunately I knew what that was, but it didn't entirely reassure me and I still could not get an overview of the impact of this personal project. That too turned out better than expected. The desire was

House HdF, 2007-2011

for a house where the garden could be experienced from the inside and thus with a close relationship between inside and outside. At quarter to seven this morning the polder was still enveloped in mist. Now it's ten o'clock and I'm sitting on my 80cm-high platform, with the sliding doors open, looking at the garden where the trees stand out against a vivid blue sky. It worked! I wanted to keep the house limited in materials and colours, knowing that black and white are my favourites. Only grey has been added. I could cope with that much compromise, so that worked too. And it has to 'feel' like a suit by a Japanese designer who's dear to my heart. Even more than that, the footprint of the house is a Y.

On one quarter of the plot, the house stands planted between standard fruit trees, is surrounded by a windbreak and is only discovered after passing through an ordinary gate and going down a meandering path. Unpaved of course. The view of the house is obscured by the barn, and then suddenly you have the confrontation that still silences me every day. The first glimpse of something you don't expect there.

For me, the 'when' was an exercise in patience and peacefulness, but also amazed anticipation. I had to weather two annoying winters and lots of craftsmen, without catalogues, as everything was tailor-made. The same meticulousness as in the design stage emerged here too, and many a time the execution was tested for its consistency with the design. Perseverance and endurance are welcome qualities at such times. Having a budget does not guarantee the price, but is more like a summary of the activities still to be performed.

191

But then, in the end, and on the 'day of the family', we were able to move in and make the house our home.

The house no longer had to be won over while we lived in it. That had already happened during the discussion of the plans (and sub-plans) and execution of the work. In this final period, changes occurred in my personal life that fundamentally modified the original principle of the home, though it

definitely did not become a home for the elderly. On the contrary. Every part of the house is put to the test and comes through with flying colours.

Ever since the first day I lived here I have felt at home, secure, and I enjoy every line, interior view and view to the outside. Thank you Marie-José, with your unfailing zeal to make something as fine as this and for being so extremely consistent in your ideas.

A farmyard with an orchard, moat, and 19th century barn formed the starting point for this commission. The dilapidated farmhouse on the street didn't offer enough privacy and was therefore demolished, with the cellar retained to serve as a sunken and sheltered terrace. The neglected terrain was cleared of all non-native greenery, and new indigenous shrubs and trees were planted in order to create a dense border.

One of the earliest design intentions was to respond to the height of both the existing tall elm trees and the barn with its impressive roof, as well as to command views over the surrounding landscape and towards the sea on the horizon. Planning restrictions meant that the new dwelling could not exceed the 850 cubic metre volume of the original farmhouse. As a result, the upper floor levels have a smaller floor plan, in order to reach the required height, while at the same time reducing the overall volume.

The new house takes the form of a tall, concrete volume, twelve metres high, that is flanked on the ground floor by two single-storey, timber-framed wings, which angle from the base of the concrete tower to create a Y-shaped ground floor plan. This Y-shape is the result of a long search to establish connections between the house and all corners of the site, so that the surrounding terrain can enter the house from three sides.

The house was repositioned at the rear of the site in order to maximise views towards the garden and orchard, while reorienting the ground floor towards the south allows sunshine to fully permeate the interior.

The main access to the house lies recessed between two wings, where a covered entrance shelters against strong North Sea winds. The vestibule forms part of the circulation core in the northwest corner of the

1/5000

house, from where a timber staircase winds upwards through the house around a lift.

The living and dining areas on the ground floor face south towards the orchard and are elevated at a height of 80 centimetres above the level of the ground outside. They feature glazed walls which can open fully onto a raised and covered terrace, or *engawa*, which is at the same floor height and has the effect of extending the interior outwards, to visually and spatially connect the house with the garden.

The positioning of a double-sided, freestanding hearth in the centre of the ground floor helps to organise the space by delineating and framing different areas. It distinguishes the living area from the dining room, which in turn is separated from the kitchen by a storage room.

A geometrically-sculpted concrete chimney rises up from the hearth, forming the spine to which the upper floors are attached. Continuing on above roof level, the end of the chimney becomes a turret, marking the pinnacle of the vertical concrete volume.

On the first floor, the main bedroom looks out over the garden and pebbled roof. The shower room situated above the entrance pierces the concrete volume with a bay window, enhancing the contact with nature at the start of one's day. A bathroom and children's bedroom (which was originally conceived as a library) are located on the second floor. From here, a staircase leads to the roof terrace, arranged on two levels. A notch cut into the high concrete parapet on the sea-facing side reinforces the idea of a lookout tower, inviting one to gaze out at the

containerships on the horizon when the weather allows.

A bright-coloured, architectural concrete was chosen for the tower, to correspond to the sandy beaches of the nearby coast (Cadzand, the most southerly seaside town in the Netherlands, lies 3 kilometres away). The finished surface of the concrete was formed by horizontally placing wooden planks as shuttering, with the marks of these planks remaining clearly visible.

The same language was repeated in the vertically-placed, blackened wooden planks that cover the façade of the ground floor timber-framed volumes, and refers to the historical use of planking in the construction of the barns in the surrounding area. The black and white stained joinery of the windows also directly references the local vernacular.

1 covered entrance
2 vestibule
3 kitchen
4 storage room
5 dining room
6 seating area
7 engawa
8 lift
9 cellar entrance
10 bedroom
11 wardrobe
12 shower room
13 bedroom/library
14 bathroom
15 hearth
16 terrace

MMV – 02
House and doctor's practice
Van Aelten – Oosterlinck, Opwijk, 2005-2011

Swimming pond and pool house, 2014-2016

The house is situated in the heart of a village, where the church tower in the background is one of the few buildings of historical character that remain. It was a challenge to integrate the relatively large building programme – a dwelling with four bedrooms, practice room and parking space – into the small-scale fabric.

The difficulties of the site determine the building. The deep plot, with a large garden, folds with a kink towards the street, which bounds the site to the south. In addition, right to light easement regulations affect the site in relation to the neighbour on the left. The 'unwritten' urban development rules permit garages and garden pavilions to be built at the back of the plot, on the garden side, but residential functions are not permitted in that zone.

The house extends over the site and unfolds along a sequence of inner courtyards. The entrance to the front door on the side of the street is reached through the first of these enclosed outdoor areas, which is partly covered to create a carport. Behind it the house folds to the shape of the plot, and kinks away from the zone protected by the right to light easement. This kink gives shape to a second, larger outdoor area, a central patio at the heart of the house, around which most of the act of dwelling takes place. This patio allows the living spaces that extend along it to be oriented towards the south, thereby enjoying a maximum of sunlight. A third, smaller courtyard creates a separation between the dwelling and the practice room, and brings light into the basement level of the house.

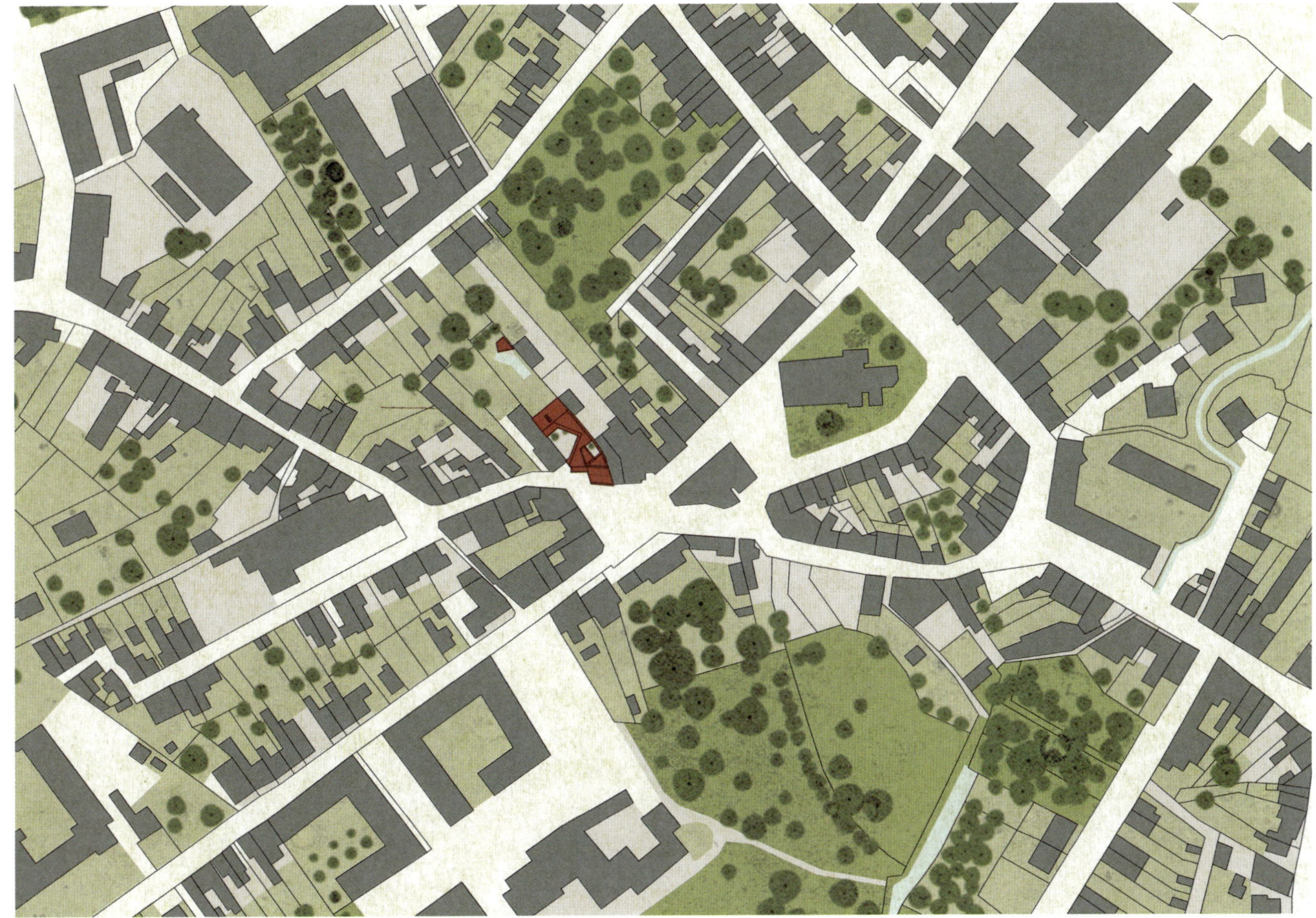

1/2500

Two different paths lead to the back garden. The first route runs through the interior of the house, along the windows of the various inner courtyards. The second route is through the exterior spaces, via covered passages that connect one courtyard to the next.

The passage between the largest patio and the back garden runs alongside a small shower room. In the warmer half of the year this block is left open, since the roof offers sufficient shelter. In the winter it is closed off by sliding doors.

A solid wood staircase winds up to the sleeping area on the street side, changing direction every time it arrives at one of the four landings that each lead to a bedroom. The parents' bedroom is tucked under the roof, and opens onto a large roof terrace at the rear of the house. On the upper levels, a narrow internal terrace separates the building from the neighbour to the right. This offers the opportunity to place discrete windows in the adjacent bathrooms, which overlook the private terrace.

Recently, a rectilinear swimming pool was excavated at the deepest part of the garden, folding along its length with a slight kink. An almost square-shaped pool house with a sauna and storage forms the end point of the plot. This wooden house is, as it were, wrapped in a concrete shell.

The brick used for the façades is a familiar material that relates to the surrounding houses in the village. Due to the thick cement joints in the simple brick pattern, the material here becomes more abstract. The roof tiles made from fired clay also recall the materials found in the locality. The flooring of the exterior courtyards is formed by irregular polygons in washed concrete. Openings have been left between these stone slabs, allowing nature to recolonise the courtyards through the growth of vegetation along the edges and the joints.

The interior has also been completely designed by Van Hee; staircases with solid wood treads, the kitchen, the wardrobes in the bedrooms, study desks for the children's bedrooms, the practice room and the office for the inhabitants. Furniture becomes floor-to-ceiling walls. When closed, they conceal the inevitable clutter of daily life. Then the perimeters that determine the architecture take precedence: the different window frames, the joints in the terrazzo floor, the articulation of the passageways – with pivoting wooden doors either open or not – the generous, flowing space.

1 entrance
2 private entrance
3 waiting room
4 practice
5 study
6 carport
7 bicycle storage
8 seating area
9 kitchen
10 shower room
11 bathroom
12 garden storage
13 courtyard
14 patio
15 garden
16 archive
17 storage
18 laundry
19 terrace
20 bedroom
21 covered passage

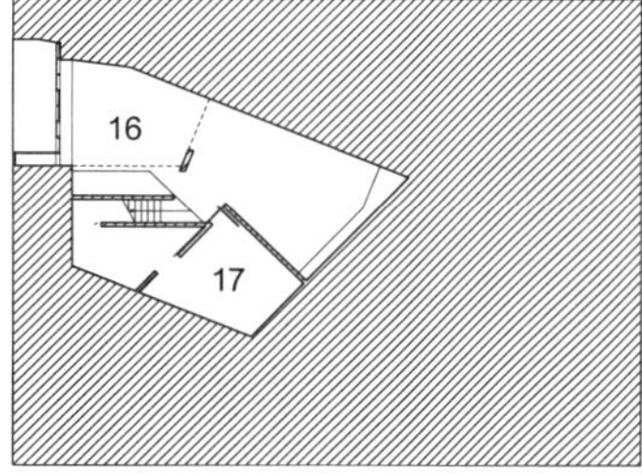

basement plan

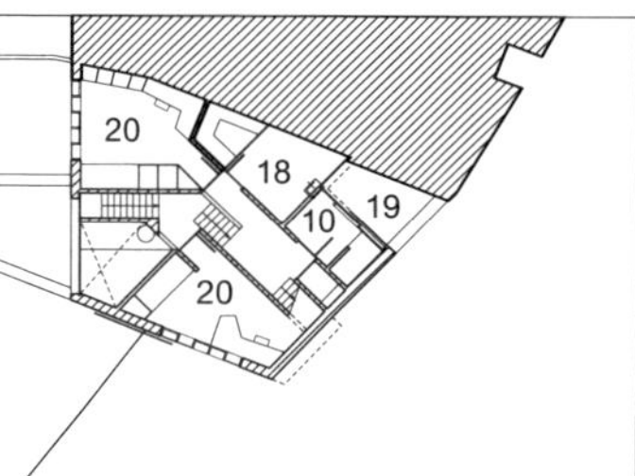

first floor plan

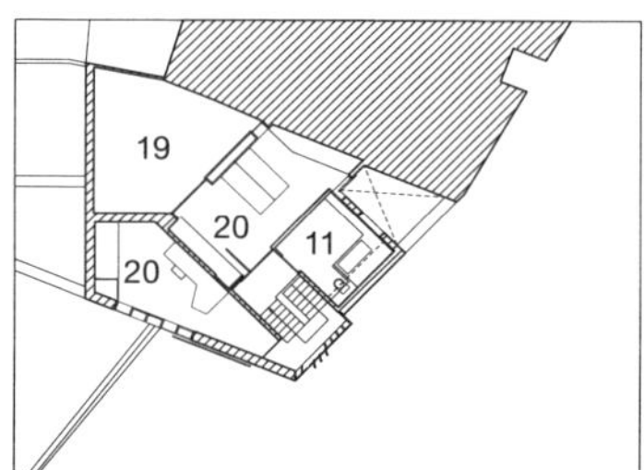

second floor plan

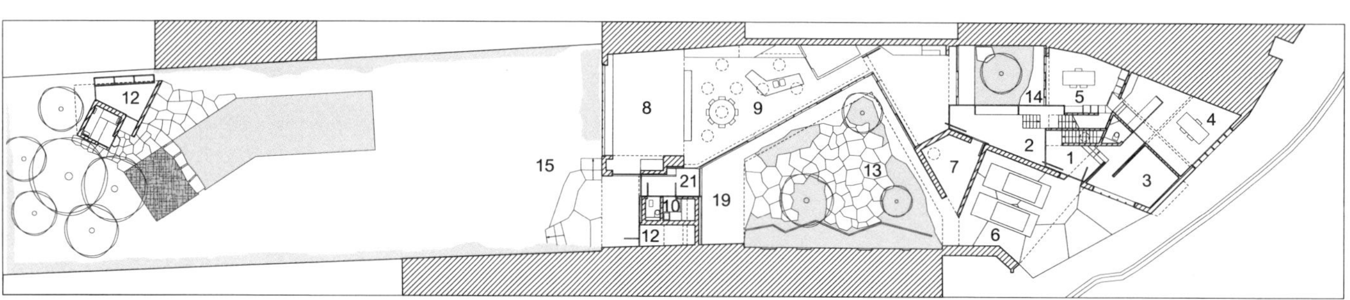

ground floor plan

0　5　10　15 m

Tactile and reflective conditions in the architecture of Marie-José Van Hee

Javier Fernández Contreras

The side of the smooth green hill, torn by floods, may at first very properly be called deformed; and on the same principle, though not with the same impression, as a gash on a living animal. When a rawness of such a gash in the ground is softened, and in part concealed and ornamented by the effects of time, and the progress of vegetation, deformity by this usual process, is converted into picturesqueness; and this is the case with quarries, gravel pits, etc., which at first are deformities, and which in their most picturesque state, are often considered as such by a levelling improver.
Sir Uvedale Price. *Essays on the Picturesque*, Vol. 1.
(London: J.G. Barnard, 1810) p. 195.

A first look at the material library at the office of Marie-José Van Hee as it stands today reveals a quest for material authenticity. The meeting table in the centre is guarded by a collection of samples which is very telling of the conditions with which the architect associates physicality. The library is even more revealing for what it lacks than for what it possesses. In an era of industrially processed 'perfect' products, it displays an array of handcrafted and seemingly imperfect materials.

The absence of plastics and metals, the limited presence of glass and the preference for solid bricks with no signs of vitrification nor any other kind of superficial modification seem to articulate an argument against the effects of industrialisation. The choice of Delft tiles, which always result in subtle, sequin-like surfaces that exhibit a lack of homogeneity in their colour, superficiality and edges, indicates a preference for soft variation and textured reality. Even in the shelves reserved for wood, despite the presence of a few laminated blocks, it is raw solidity that dominates, as if influenced by the grey pieces of stone nearby.

House Lowie-Derks, 1983-1986

House Van Hee-Coppens, 1990-1993

If we turn around, the picture is no different, yet in this case it is the elevation, the face of materials, that takes prominence over other aspects. The terrazzo and the fabrics seem to possess a special intensity of colour, and in the way they display their grain, the wooden panels acquire a transparent and multi-faceted condition, dexterously achieved through successive layers of primer and a richly pigmented paint. Ultimately, this material library represents the conviction that it is the tactile, material and physical condition of architecture that determines its experience.

OPENING MOVEMENTS: FROM SYMBOLIC VOLUMES TO HUMANISED INTERIOR SPACES

The main façade of Marie-José Van Hee's first fully independent work, the Lowie-Derks House, developed from 1983 to 1986, bears a resemblance to those of her postmodern contemporaries in the iconicity of its pitched-roof, the symmetrical array of windows and the gable at the front, but the architect's real intentions are unveiled inside, through the embodiment of an interior domain freed from any linguistic connotations, driven exclusively by the experience of space. The contrast between the exterior image of the house, still embedded in the symbolism of its time, whose character can be easily reflected through photography, and the sophistication of an interior space whose humanism can only be experienced through a direct visit, really set the tone for the rest of Van Hee's career.

The exterior photograph shows an adjacent building, its curtains shielding the interior from the curiosity of passers-by. In the Lowie-Derks House, the subtle decision to raise the ground floor a few steps with respect to the street level avoids the necessity for corrective mechanisms such as curtains for the interior's privacy. The house demonstrates aspects of the architecture of Van Hee that would become characteristic of her language: the idea that the connection to the street brings in light but not a direct visual communication, which is produced on the contrary towards the garden; the decided vocation to slenderise daylight and frame it vertically, showing ultimately a taste for overhead light coming from vertical planes; or the interior stair that ascends weightlessly in a canonical image of her architecture, linking all floors vertically with no need to incorporate the surrounding rooms visually.

Yet it is in the intensity of a living room which unfolds into the garden that Van Hee's understanding of interior space is revealed, specifically her position on the interaction between house and site. The array of tiles in the courtyard and the naturalistic approach to the structure of vegetation create the right conditions for this seemingly natural landscape to develop, turning the garden into the first source of a tactile experience.

The project also shows early explorations into the interplay between texture and surface in her architecture. Whereas the white walls inside the house are homogeneously flat, the façade and walls around the courtyard display a thick layer of brushed cement coat. Yet this transition does not occur automatically: between the load-bearing wall of the façade and the concrete frame structure inside the house, there lies a recessed intermediate space reserved for a thick curtain, a source of tangible materiality whose presence is always shielded in Van Hee's projects, revealing that this is an architecture that enjoys the tectonic encounters, the physicality of construction and, ultimately, the ephemeral stability of reality.

Marie-José Van Hee likes to design architecture from the inside, conceiving interior spaces with a sense of classicism in the proportions, a mastery in the use of daylight and an accomplished use of

House Van Hee, 1994-1997

Market Hall, 1996–2012

contemporary construction techniques. Other projects from this first era of her career operate on the same principles regarding the interior space, but show a gradual abandonment of symbolic conditions, mainly through the progressive abstraction of the architectural volume and the further exploration of dynamic forms of interior space, a quest in which echoes of *Wrightian* compositions resonate as clearly as the interest of the architect in the *Loosian* raumplan.

Commenced five years later, the Pay House presents a volume of assembled prisms and slender vertical windows that would become distinctive features of Van Hee's emerging style. By shaping the showroom and domestic space with intersecting perpendicular walls, the folds of the perimeter break up the volume in successive contractions that create diagonal visual connections between front and back, in a scheme of inspiring emotion and poetic formal strength.

Begun in 1990, the Van Hee-Coppens House is the coherent culmination of the experiments of the '80s. The project unfolds in a sequence of staggered horizontal prisms, centripetal walls and vertical windows whose mullions create an interplay of light and shadow. 'Light is a material for me, I don't like frameless glass panes,' Van Hee would recall in a conversation with the author. The construction's asymmetrical scheme in the landscape renders the interiors of the house more fluid, where the architect once again shows her ability to integrate house and garden through intersecting volumes, horizontal canopies and exterior galleries, qualities that in the next episode of her career would be intensified by a deeper experimentation with the material condition of architecture.

VARKENSSTRAAT AND MARKET HALL: PATINA OF TIME VERSUS ATMOSPHERIC REFLECTIONS

Van Hee's own private house at Varkensstraat was commenced in 1994, marking a transition in her work from solid flat surfaces and spaces to an idea of deep materials and textured reality. Whereas there has been a considerable amount of discussion about layered façades in recent decades, Van Hee's understanding of depth here applies to all architectural surfaces, whether interior or exterior, and impregnates architectural space itself. At Varkensstraat, the masonry walls of the façades are cement coated but clearly show the texture of bricks; the timber beams of the living room's ceiling are painted in black but still reveal the wood grain; and the concrete columns of the gallery around the courtyard are imprinted with the pattern of the wooden formwork, creating a vivid texture that sizzles with daylight. There is a millimetric understanding of surface conditions. Those first millimetres that the hand can reach and feel, seem to be critical for Van Hee. Ultimately, there is a quest for abstract spaces with tactile textures.

Whereas in picturesque architecture, the roughness of newness requires time to be softened, this is an architecture that seems to instantly incorporate the patina of time. This, along with Van Hee's apparent lack of interest in the composition of elevations, renders architecture timeless. This is an attitude that impregnates space itself: in her own house, the change of structure between the courtyard's gallery and the living room makes it hard to ascertain what was built first. The articulation between surface and space renders the courtyard indispensable. This creates a sense of tactile proximity, and finally an awareness of the phenomenal effects of architectural surfaces.

The radical decision to divide the courtyard into two parts turns the dividing brick wall into a canvas of accelerated time, always reachable with the eye view. The wall is, in short, a photosensitive plate that endlessly records what happens around it: the weather phenomena, the passing of time and the naturalisation of the garden. This canvas is never old nor new, wet nor dry, but it fundamentally embodies all these conditions simultaneously. Traditional surface flatness is abandoned in favour of deep textural emotions.

This seems to be true even of the iconic Market Hall in Ghent, a project co-authored by Marie-José Van Hee and Robbrecht en Daem architecten, begun in 1996 and built between 2011 and 2012. Even though the building has a monumental presence and a sense of formal continuity with the pitched roofs of the adjacent medieval constructions, it is the careful selection of roof materials that brings a detached yet contextual object back to the city.

A seemingly gigantic vernacular shed rests on four massive concrete columns, creating a public space in the place of formerly demolished medieval buildings. Whereas there is a sense of stitching in the urban scar, the roof structure praises its prominence through the atmospheric incorporation of context. If the house at Varkensstraat celebrates the accumulation of density through the patina of time, the Market Hall exhibits a display of continuous variability: the stratification of the roof materials – steel, wood and glass – causes the weather and light conditions to unceasingly transform its volume, altering its texture and resonating in it through the delicate performativity of the glass, a material that is at the same time transparent and reflective, invisible and contextual.

The decision to leave the concrete columns with a perfect industrial finish renders the building weightless thanks to the contrast with the almost primitive wooden shed above. The change of materiality in the side elevations, where glass is abandoned, and from there to the inside, which resembles a golden coffer at night, reinforces this performative and unstable condition.

The Market Hall incorporates in its reflections and refractions the architectural and topological silhouettes of Ghent, mirroring at each moment a different city, each of them real. Unlike previous projects, whose materiality seems unresponsive to energetic conditions, the construction here looks different depending on both the season and time of day. The layered shell makes use of this disjunction between the inner and outer skin to generate compound visual effects of material reflections and city atmospheres, transforming the project into a gigantic piece of gravitational equilibrium.

ULTIMATE QUEST: GRAMMAR OF TACTILE TECTONICS, SPACE OF LAYERED TRANSPARENCY
The Market Hall parallels to some extent a culminant genealogy of projects by Van Hee that shows a transition from the experimental effects of tactile surfaces to the subtle nuances of layered transparencies. Started in 2003, the Anné-Buyl House displays a sense of vernacular monumentality in its proportions. The front façade explicitly reveals in its disciplined composition of doors and windows the architectural attributes of a house, whereas the back elevation integrates the solid brickwork of the façade with a large glazed surface, creating an interesting balance between the language of modern rural architecture and that of a traditional greenhouse.

Whereas this construction seems to mirror the architecture of the adjacent vernacular pavilion, the grammar is different. The horizontal mullion of the glass veranda is aligned with the cornice of the adjacent construction, yet the proportions and transparencies are monumentalised. There is even a sense that the rules of gravity and perspective

House Anné-Buyl, 2003-2007

are transformed, and that what before was easy to read vertically, from the ridge on top to the greenery in front of the house, is now complex to read in depth. The gravitational condition of the house is distorted, endowing it with an atmospheric condition.

This is even true for renovation projects, where Van Hee shows a great talent for transforming constrictions into assets. At the Steel House, an intervention into an existing building carried out from 2000 to 2003, it seems that the work of the architect consists mainly in eliminating redundant elements and clearing up the space until an open plan scheme is achieved. The ground floor of the house is opened up and beautifully articulated with the backyard through an asymmetrical glass façade. This is a space diagram that Van Hee has been confidently developing for years: the house presents narrow, subtle openings towards the outside world, and spills out onto the landscape at the back.

Declercq House, one of Marie-José Van Hee's latest projects, delves into the previous experiments of Anné-Buyl and Steel houses and opens up a culminating chapter in the interplay between tactile and reflective conditions in her architecture. From the outside, the house reveals a simple construction embodying all the categories traditional domesticity is associated with: a ceramic pitched roof is punctuated by a chimney that explicitly symbolises the warmth of the home, a brick masonry wall is topped by a gutter that shows how rainwater is collected and drained, and a flat grass esplanade in front of the house creates a bucolic, almost pastoral, experience.

Originally a renovation of two vernacular houses, this is a construction that seems to belong to a time of imperfect physicality. The different degrees of baking of the roof tiles, the wandering horizontality of the roof ridge and the texture of a brickwork technically distinct from the machine ambitions of early modernism, all display a handmade craftsmanship with a sense of gravity and primitivism. The proportions of the pitched roof and those of the windows take us back to a time long before the structural darings of contemporary architecture: a time when the carrying of the loads was readable, architectural materials were authentic and landscape was natural. Even the wooden window frames, whose mullions create a 3x3 checkerboard, seem to hark back to days when glass could not be conceived as a continuous flat surface. As it stands, the building could even be identified as an icon of old domesticity. Yet a closer look at the house reveals a deeper reality than this elevation suggests.

If we attempt to peer inside the windows, none of them reveal the predictable elements the inside of a house should be expected to contain. As if it were a *trompe l'oeil*, each of them shows a different reality. Whereas the window on the right remains dark and reflective, the middle one reveals a bucolic landscape with some domestic elements in front, conveniently replaced by a swimming pool of hedonic condition on the left one. None of these elements can be seen at our back, which eliminates any chance of this being a reflection. One is even reminded of a surrealistic composition *à la belge*, with that *Magrittian* genius for the interplay between super realistic, almost ordinary, images and surreal conditions.

The entrance of the house reveals the characteristic features of depth and surface the architect has been working on since she made her own house at Varkensstraat. The brickwork has been coated with cement mortar, a solution that creates a continuous surface enriched by the texture of the original masonry wall, and a new wooden door has been painted with successive layers of primer and varnish that reveal the wood grain. There is an archaeologic understanding of materiality on display here; a tactile condition that enjoys the accumulation of information rather than its disposal, ultimately narrating the biography of the building.

House Declercq, 2014–2018

House Declercq, 2014-2018

Inside the house, the game of perception is revealed. The load-bearing masonry wall opposite that of the entrance façade has been replaced by a floor-to-ceiling wooden frame glass elevation that renders the landscape transparent. The scenery that was previously framed and reticulated now unravels naturally, with the greenery in front, the swimming pool on the left and a *Barragánian* wall on the right. These were all existing elements, yet the perception of them has been altered. Floor-to-ceiling sliding doors are on the one hand sophisticated devices in keeping with an orthodox view of modernism, but on the other, they can be read as a complete abstraction of the tactile, material basis of architecture. This implies a malleable interior-exterior relationship, and a definition of the interior that is far richer than the mere observation of an existing reality.

The *trompe l'oeil* seems to have been revealed at once, yet this is an architecture built upon a narrative, non-simplistic condition, which enjoys the accumulation of episodes. A closer look at the surfaces here reveals how all the original tectonic elements, namely the wall and the pitched roof, have been softened. The threshold of each window does not reveal any difference between its four sides: the sill at the bottom, the lateral and the top sides are all whitewashed, blunted with a dexterous absence of joints that renders architecture ethereal, becoming a soft container in which the objects of everyday life are celebrated.

Daylight washes architectural surfaces in white, as if pretending not to be interrupted by solid, seemingly massive elements, but highlights the edges of the wooden sliding doors and those of the stone fireplace. These elements, even the furniture, explicitly show their physicality, their imperfections and joints. There is a sense of inverted tactility that plays with the senses, emotions and, essentially, perception. Whereas at the main façade there is a univocal correspondence between materiality, function and technique, underlined by the distinctive chromatic palette of the ceramic roof, the brick wall and the metallic gutter, at the back façade the interplay between materiality and function displaces the sense of meaning. The same material, hardwood of tropical origin, has been used for the load-bearing posts and the sliding doors, intelligently playing with the ambiguity of immobility and displacement.

Once outside, all elements seem to recover their literal and intrinsic character: the landscape remains green, the masonry wall recovers its brickwork texture and the roof tiles orderly convey that originally this was a piece of vernacular architecture. Yet this immediacy, as if in a final *tour de force* of perception, is finally contested by the use of glass in the back elevation. If we turn around and look inside the house from the back garden, the double condition of total transparency and reflectivity of this material creates a surface of flat depth: one is always immersed in the landscape, nature is imprisoned in glass, embedding us in a space that is at the same time flat and deep, interior and exterior, domestic and savage.

Van Hee achieves a total condition of layered space and tactile tectonics: her unadorned definition of materials creates the appearance of a domestic transparency devoid of symbolism, yet the tactile texture of the construction and the atmospheric condition of glass point to the sensory effects of architecture. The naked and essential space of the house on one side and the picturesque garden environment on the other are merged differently in the two façade walls – one solid, the other transparent – accentuating the impression caused by the reflection of figurative forms of landscape on the abstract surface of glass. Nature is not represented but displayed, enabling the observer to experience the sublime in the domestic, ultimately apprehending the world through the tactile and reflective conditions of architecture.

Along a meander of the Oude Leie, facing across the river to the sports and recreation area of Blaarmeersen, the plot boasts tall, mature trees, and until recently was occupied by a French style villa, known as 'het roze huis' because of its pink-painted façade. Prior to this, a manor house dating from 1680, *Huys van plaisance 'de Ramenas'*, had stood on the site. Early façades of the design by Marie-José Van Hee were based on an undated and unnamed painting of this manor house that had been discovered by the clients.

Two new dwellings take roughly the same positions as the most recent buildings on the site, with the larger volume of the new house lying parallel to the road, and the smaller guesthouse perpendicular. In order to maintain some distance between the new guesthouse and the neighbouring house with which it shares a party wall, an inner terrace creates a separation in the front façade, allowing the building to step up and create a higher volume at the corner furthest from the neighbour. This small tower is mirrored on the corner of the main house, on the opposite side of the courtyard that separates the two volumes, and together these two 'crowns' form a portico that high-lights the entrance to the garden beyond.

Inside the guesthouse, a stair-case leads directly up to the dwelling on the first floor, with the ground floor housing a garage and storage areas. Upstairs, a living space and kitchen look onto the inner court-yard in the front façade and open onto another terrace at the rear of the building, to which the bedroom is also attached. This first floor terrace looks out over a low wall towards the garden at the back, but facing towards the larger house on the other side of the courtyard the wall is higher and offers no direct visual connection. While there is an

1/5000

obvious relationship between the two volumes, Van Hee also felt it important that a degree of privacy was respected between the two dwellings.

A large corner window wraps around the façade above the entrance to the guesthouse, allowing a direct line of sight from the rear terrace right through to the river. Likewise, from the living room you can see through the inner courtyard of the front façade to the white gable wall of the neighbouring house, as well as across to Blaarmeersen on the other side of the river. Such connections represent a recurring theme and important element in Van Hee's work: the idea of duality, between open and closed, between inside and outside.

Across the courtyard, the main dwelling is entered through a covered overhang, which draws you inwards to arrive at a spacious, high-ceilinged hall – a reception area, off which the more work-related programmes, such as the meeting room and office, are found. Storage and laundry areas act as a buffer between this outer, more public zone, and the inner, more private, family-oriented part of the house. The main family room, a vast space measuring 8 by 19 metres, is characterised by wooden beams that run the entire width of the ceiling, and a large, sculptural fireplace that forms a separation between the kitchen and dining room, and the quieter seating area. The fireplace is double-sided, with a hearth on either side, but at different heights. On the side of the living room, it takes the form of a traditional fireplace, while on the side facing the kitchen and dining room, the hearth is at the height of a stove or a range, and can be used to cook. Above the kitchen worktops and cabinets, a slender canopy floats one metre below the underside of the ceiling beams, creating a more domestic, intimately scaled room within a room that is reminiscent of St. Jerome's *studiolo* in the painting by Antonello da Messina.

Since the garden along the street to the front of the house is northwest facing, with the rear garden facing southeast, the approach has been to fragment the views and connections towards the front garden, while maximising those towards the rear. As a result, the façade towards the street is more classically proportioned, with four equally-sized, vertical windows on the ground level. The walls between these windows are doubled in thickness by cupboards fitted on the inside, which, as well as providing

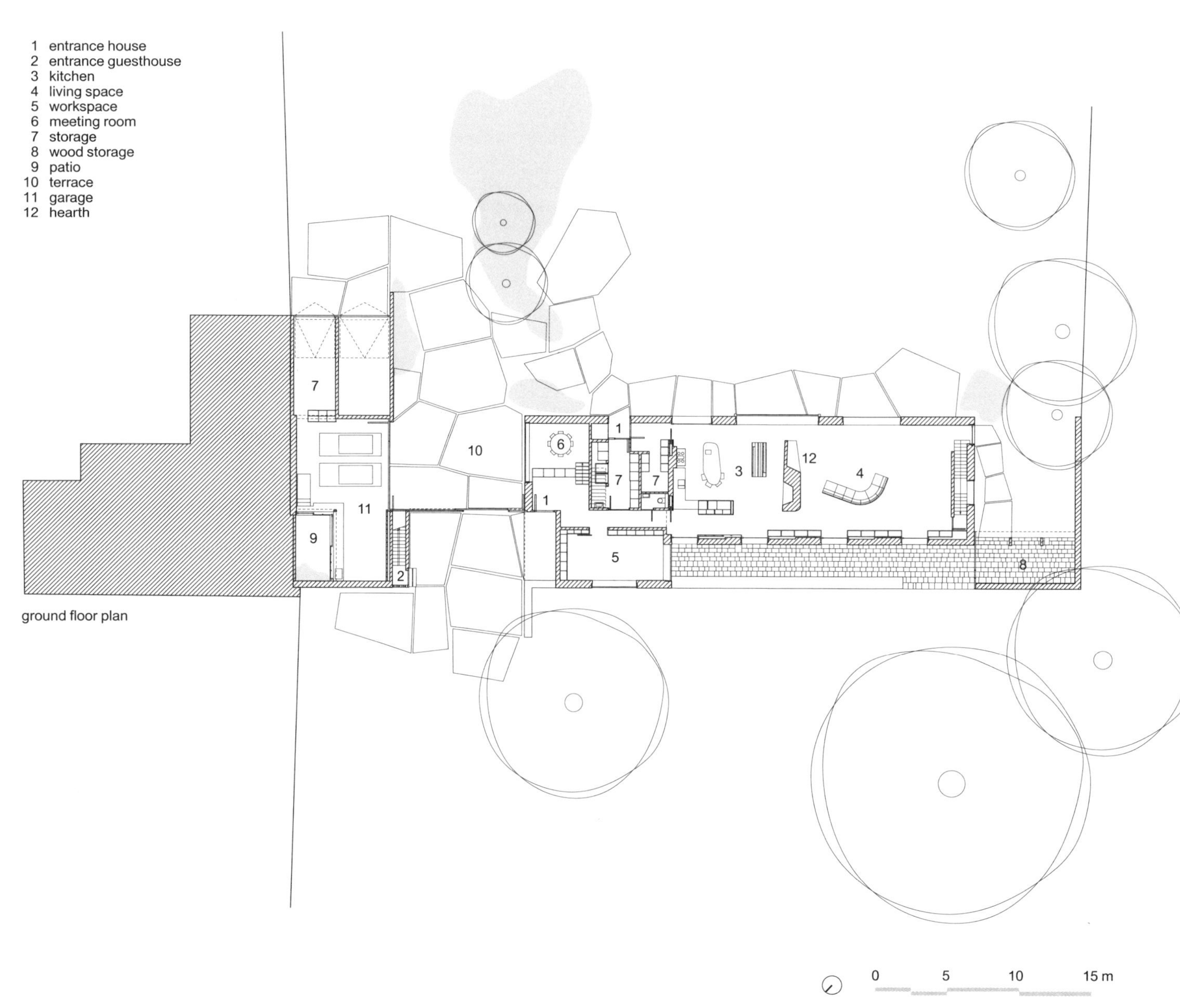

ground floor plan

storage, conveniently conceal the horizontally-sliding shutters for the windows.

At the rear elevation, a pergola runs along the ground floor façade, the structure of which is incorporated into the brickwork of the façade, with steel fins extending from the masonry to support wooden lattice work. Intended to eventually be overgrown with greenery, this pergola extends outwards by around one metre at the end closest to the kitchen, but extends more than twice as far at the other end, where the pavement which runs along the house also widens to form a larger patio. A huge window behind the fireplace, six metres wide and almost three metres in height, can slide fully open to connect the main room with the garden beyond.

While the ground floor of the rear façade is in solid brick masonry, the first floor is constructed in wood. The contrast between the heavier lower storey and lighter upper storey – where the sleeping quarters have been slotted into position, wooden boxes sitting atop the brick volume – recalls the hybrid construction of the Smithsons' Upper Lawn Pavilion, in which a zinc-clad, wooden framed box was built on top of an existing stone garden wall. All of the bedrooms open onto a terrace, with the top of the brick parapet doubling as a balustrade.

Urban development regulations were particularly restrictive with respect to the height of the roof, so in order to create a higher profile, Van Hee confides with a smile, 'we have played a little game in the cornice.' An elegant bronze-coloured steel profile that adorns the top of both buildings like a crown, the cornice serves to refine the otherwise simple volumes, performing at the same time other functions: it is the flashing for the brick parapets; it forms the roof profile for the wooden structures; and most remarkably, at the furthest corner of the main house, it cantilevers over the first floor terrace to create a delicately floating border that frames the sky.

Finding the right brick to use for the façades involved a long search. It was originally intended to use the same recuperated bricks as the garden wall for the houses, but procuring the necessary amount proved impossible. In the end, a brick was found that was of the same, slightly smaller than standard, format. The brick façades display a finely textured surface, thanks to the effect of the smaller size of the module on the *andamento*, the shimmering movement of the brick pattern. It is

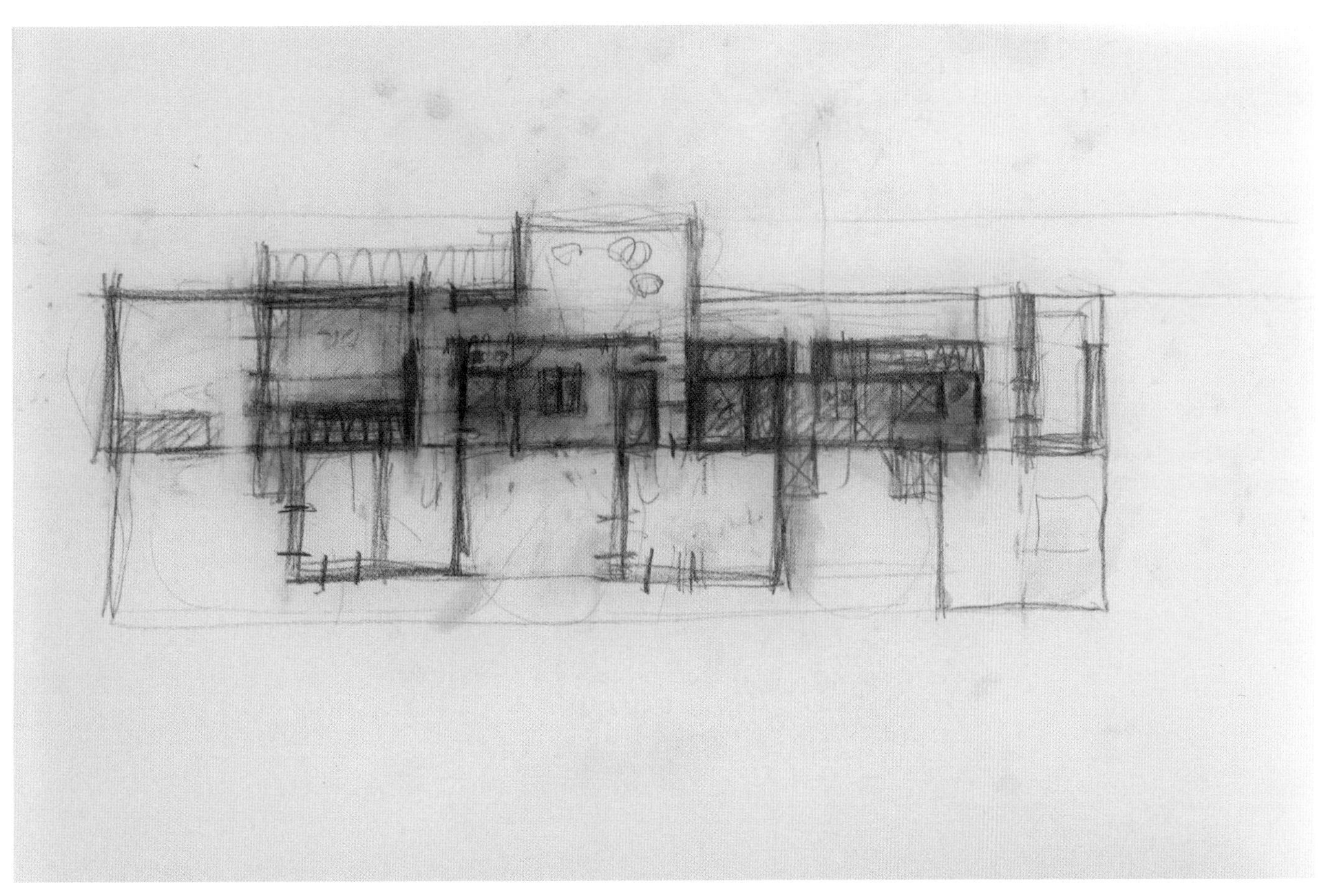

customary in houses by Marie-José Van Hee for the brick surface to be covered by a thin layer of cement slurry, an interpretation of a traditional Flemish façade finish known as *kaleien*, but when the clients saw the raw brick here, they liked it so much that they decided not to cover it up.

As a way of making openings in the brick towers without detracting from their appearance as solid volumes, honeycomb brickwork has been employed to create small perforations that dot the façades. The exact positioning of these *claustra*, as they are referred to in Dutch, was determined on site by the architects through observing how the sunlight fell. For example, the outside terrace in the parents' sleeping quarters is enclosed by high walls which offer a sense of intimacy, but these walls are executed almost entirely in honeycomb brickwork, freely punctuated by perforations. This creates an endless play of light and shadow on the stone floor of the terrace as the sun moves through the sky, and at the same time provides a link to the natural world outside, offering glimpses of the garden and the tops of the trees, and bringing the cycle of the seasons into the life of the interior.

The garden wall that surrounds the orchard also encloses the swimming pool and pool house, which are positioned on what Van Hee describes as the most *luw* area of the garden, *een luwe plek* being a place with no wind, but also enjoying abundant sunlight, as well as peace and quiet. Here again, another game has been played with the cornice, this time in order to break up the mass and weight of the roof. There are in fact two cornices, one that incorporates the true thickness of the roof but is set back somewhat, so that the eye is drawn to a much slimmer cornice along the roof edge, which gives the impression that the entire roof canopy is only a fraction of its actual thickness.

The terrace of the pool, like the plinth at the front of the main house, is in limestone, as are the massive, oversized steps at each end. Under the canopy of the pool house, the horizontal opening of the hearth is reflected at a 45 degree angle in an aperture cut into the perpendicular wall, creating an unexpected connection to a shaded passage that runs between the site boundary and the garden wall, a counterpoint to the sunny poolside terrace. This aperture is once again repeated at the furthest end of the pool house, in a wide, horizontal opening above

a concrete bench that permits shafts of sunlight to enter the interior, at the same time beautifully framing the theatrical figures of the fruit trees in the orchard, in a scene from Valerius De Saedeleer.

When creating views out to the garden, Van Hee likes to work with diagonals: 'in this way you lengthen the space, in this case doubling the dimension of the garden – straight lines of vision tend to foreshorten, whereas diagonal views elongate the space and give a feeling of more depth'. This has been something of a fascination since her graduation thesis exploring the gardens of the south, where she wandered in her imagination through the sequences and passages of the gardens at the Villa d'Este in Tivoli.

The idea of passage, the richness of experience in moving through spaces that continually expand and contract, with views opening and closing, brings to mind what Gordon Cullen referred to as *Serial Vision*. Marie-José Van Hee compares directing and framing views in architecture to how a director or cinematographer frames their shot: 'just like in filmmaking, you create the setting for a scene, and from a series of scenes you form a sequence. Before I used to think that architecture was simply about building, placing block upon block, but now more and more I see that it is also about scenography.'

MMIX – 14
Refurbishment of the Market Square, road infrastructure, Reinbachplein, public space and Leie riverbanks, Deinze, 2009 – ongoing

Historical maps of Deinze from the late 18th century clearly show the principle components which defined the city centre and served to organise the urban space. The most obvious and important of these can be read as the course and position of the River Leie; the perpendicular axis of the market place, which stretches from the river towards the canal to the north; and the green space of the former fortifications, lying parallel along the market's length. The re-establishment of these elements – the market square as a stone parcours linking the two waterways, with a green meander running parallel along one side – formed the starting point for the redevelopment by Marie-José Van Hee architecten in collaboration with Robbrecht en Daem architecten. Based on a masterplan by uapS (Anne Mie Depuydt and Erik Van Daele), it structures the space on three levels: it creates a public square with monuments and public buildings, it strengthens the relationship with the river, and traffic flow is rerouted to make more room for people.

While the market square has served various purposes throughout the ages – it hosts a weekly market held every Wednesday since at least the 15th century, an open-air theatre for the Canteclaer parade, a horse fair still held every 4 years, and the Deinze festival – over the last few decades it had become first and foremost a functional space, mainly given over to traffic circulation and parking. In terms of public realm, the prioritisation of cars had been to the detriment of the flexible and all-inclusive character of the square, and a total reorganisation was needed in order for it to once more become an accessible and useable space for the people of Deinze.

Van Hee often refers to historical documents as a way to gain an

1/6000

insight into a site or project: 'I look at what was there before – what was good about it, why it was good – and ask if it might be worth bringing something of that back.' In this case, a 19th century postcard showing the market square as a broad, open space that stretched unobstructed from one side of the street to the other, served to point a way forward, by revealing the previously coherent and open character of the space before it had been eroded by the arrival and predominance of the motorcar.

To rectify the imbalance between cars and other users, vehicular traffic on the market square has now been limited to one lane, and parking spaces have been greatly reduced. The laying of an even, uniform paving in a grey-brown sandstone has eliminated all level differences and created a plaza that

once again stretches from façade to façade: an open, flat surface, free from any obstacles, accessible for people of all mobilities and offering much more flexibility in terms of possible uses.

The next strategic action focused on visually shortening the 600 metre length of the market place, in order to create a more readable and manageable distance for a person travelling on foot. As Van Hee points out, 'The scale of a car and the scale of a person are completely different, as are the speeds at which they move – while a car could drive from one end of the market square to the other in one or two minutes, a person walking would take ten minutes. That's why in order to have a more human scale, the distance needed to be broken up again … we wanted

to break the monotony, create a sequence, shorten the distance.'

The view along a long, straight road quickly becomes monotonous, whereas the distance seems to decrease if one encounters points of interest and changes of scenery along the route. With this in mind, the market square was split in a clear division into two squares centred on a pivot point, a roundabout at which the position of the road switches from one side to the other.

Four large areas of colour have been introduced within the paving, a rhythm of contrasting elements that further divide the length of the market into recognisable spaces by drawing attention to important historical buildings along the square. Created in collaboration with artist Benoît van Innis, they act as forecourts, being positioned at the entrances to Onze-Lieve-

Precedent study colourfield 'Winter' by Benoît van Innis

Vrouwekerk, the library next to the former city hall, a new canopy, and Huis Van Thuyne. These areas of colour reference the painters of the Leie region, and were inspired by their paintings of the four seasons that hang in the Museum of Deinze, with compositions in green, yellow and blue, red and orange, and black and white depicting spring, summer, autumn and winter.

Other elements have been integrated into these coloured planes: for example, the fountains outside the library invite children to play on warmer days, and thereby reinforce the identity and recognition of the theme of summer. Halfway along the length of the market square beside the pivot point, a new canopy has been constructed over the recently unearthed foundations of the original Belfry of Deinze,

which dated from the 13th century but was destroyed by fire in 1792. This urban roof represents autumn through the form of an overhanging tree, with the columns representing tree trunks, a pattern of yellow and red leaves on the underside of the roof, and fallen leaves in the pavement below. The canopy acts as a focal point, a milestone marking the halfway stage, and provides a covered space for markets, events, or concerts.

These forecourts have also created opportunities to connect the market place more closely with its surroundings. Huis Van Thuyne, for instance, acts as a new public entrance gate to Kaandelpark. Announcing the theme of spring, the green of the park 'explodes' onto the market square through the green and white paved surface that radiates outwards, accen-

tuated by newly placed circular, wooden benches and groups of trees. These trees, like all those planted in the redevelopment, were laid out in groves, rather than in rows, 'because rows lengthen the distance, whereas we wanted to decrease it.'

Just past Onze-Lieve-Vrouwekerk, the market place meets the newly redesigned riverside of Leiedam at Sint-Poppoplein. Here, the cars that used to drive across the square have been rerouted and parking spaces removed in order to reinstate Sint-Poppoplein as a space for public events. This has also allowed for the creation of two new promenades along the Leie, one at the level of the water and one at the height of the street. The riverbanks, which were for too long neglected, cut off by traffic, have been recon-

Precedent study colourfield 'Summer' (top) and 'Spring' (bottom). Paintings by Benoît van Innis

nected with the city, with the space reclaimed for people who can once again stroll along the riverfront.

A grove of trees that had previously stood between the church and the river has been replanted, edging a curved wall that accommodates the height difference between the level of the church and a new lower square that opens onto the river to the south. A long, wooden bench has been integrated into this wall, facing the Leie and perfect for enjoying the sun on a fine day. The river has been made accessible from the square via a gradually sloping deck that leads to the lower quay, with a wooden boardwalk and jetty for mooring boats.

This new boardwalk and upper promenade both continue east along Emiel Clausplein, opening onto another newly-created smaller square at the entrance to Kalkhofstraat, further along which the new arts academy is situated.

On the other side of Sint-Poppoplein, the newly laid-out Reinbachplein forms a forecourt to a recently completed cultural and administrative centre by Tony Fretton Architects. It acts as an intersect point that brings together Leiedam, the market place, and the green meander, a leafy pathway that links the Museum of Deinze, just beyond the new administrative centre, with Kaandelpark.

At the time of writing, the project is still ongoing, and additional elements currently under construction include a car park close to Brielpoort, planted with as many trees as possible in order to ensure it becomes a continuation of the park rather than a monofunctional concrete island, and further south along the River Leie, a newly designed bridge for cyclists and pedestrians that directly links the green meander with the other side of the town.

Below the new public space of Reinbachplein with its gardens and benches, there is also a lower, more wild part of the riverbank with a gentler slope to allow ducks and other water birds to nest and access the water. A small gesture perhaps, but one that is consistent with Van Hee's approach, and her concern with the practicalities of everyday use: 'Design is not purely an exercise in aesthetics, what has been the most important consideration in this project has been use. It has been about providing a framework for people to feel good, inviting them to use and inhabit the city – and people really do use it.'

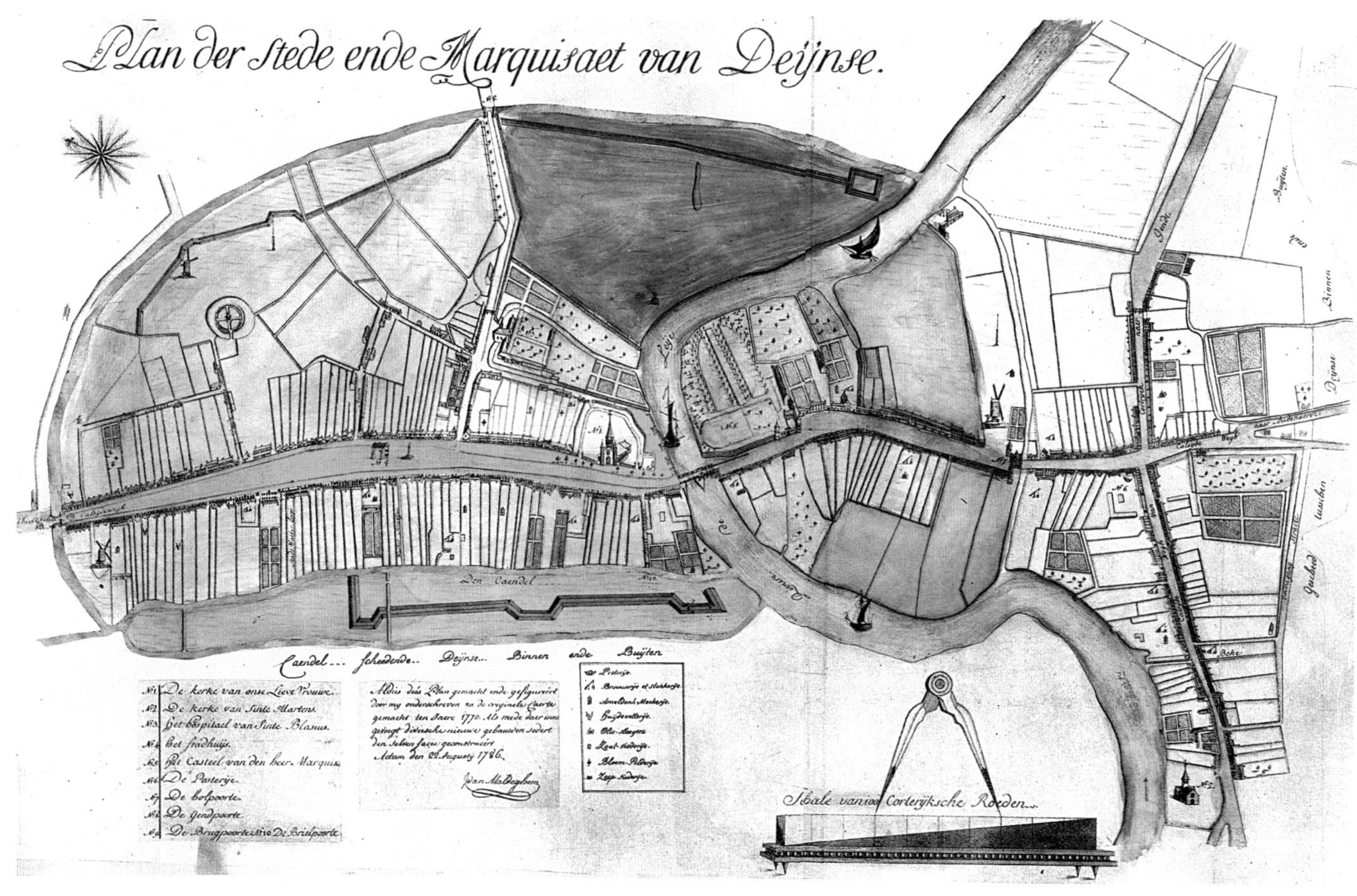

Indeed, the success of the project is evidenced by the extent to which people have embraced the new public spaces. Apart from the large crowds drawn to popular events such as fairs, concerts, and even bicycle races, on a sunny day the city is filled with people sitting on the benches, the walls, and the boardwalk. New café and restaurant terraces have appeared along the market square, and boats are docked at the jetty on Leiedam as people come and go along the river. Individual small moments made possible within a framework that encourages and enables people to use the space and make it their own, these everyday activities together serve to create an identity, defining a convivial and accommodating urban centre at the heart of Deinze.

Existing public buildings
1 Brielpoort
2 Museum van Deinze en de Leiestreek (Van Driessche, Van den Bogaerde, De Witte)
3 Onze-Lieve-Vrouwekerk
4 Former city hall and library
5 Huis Van Thuyne

New public buildings
6 Art Academy (LENS ASS with WIT)
7 Cultural centre (Trans / V+)
8 Administrative centre 'De Leie spiegel' (Tony Fretton architects)
9 Housing for the elderly OCMW Deinze (Public Centre for Social Welfare)

Public domain executed
10 Leiedam
11 Emiel Clausplein
12 Markt
13 'Winter' by Benoît van Innis
14 'Spring' by Benoît van Innis
15 'Summer' by Benoît van Innis
16 'Fall' by Benoît van Innis
17 Kaandelpark
18 Sint-Poppoplein
19 Kalkhofstraat
20 Skatepark
21 Park OCMW

Public domain tender phase
22 Reinbachplein
23 Orchard

Public domain design phase
24 Museum area with RAC parking
25 Cyclist and pedestrian bridge crossing the river Leie (Waterwegen & Zeekanaal)
26 Antoon van Paryspath
27 Cyclist and pedestrian bridge Bisschopstraat
28 Gentpoortstraat

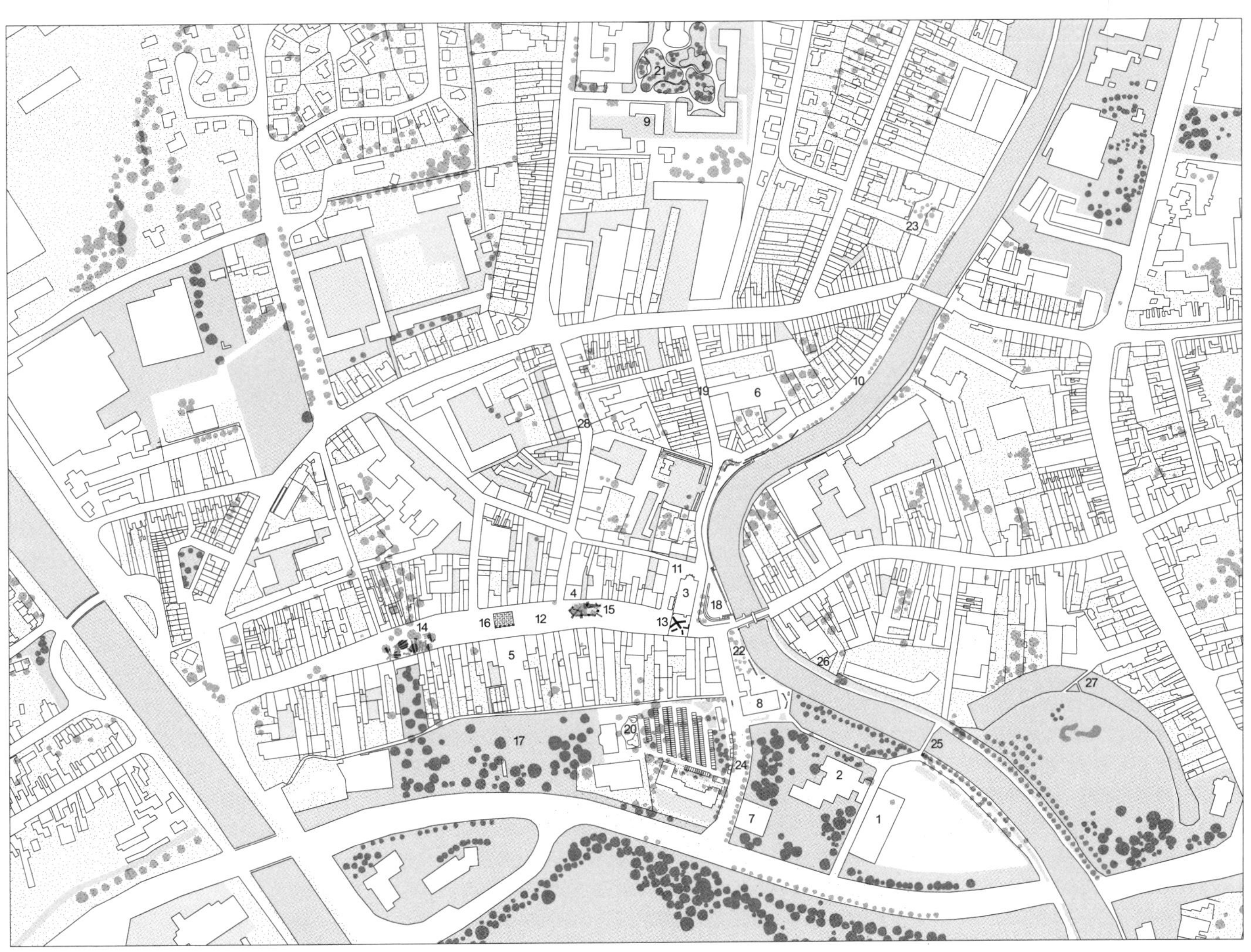

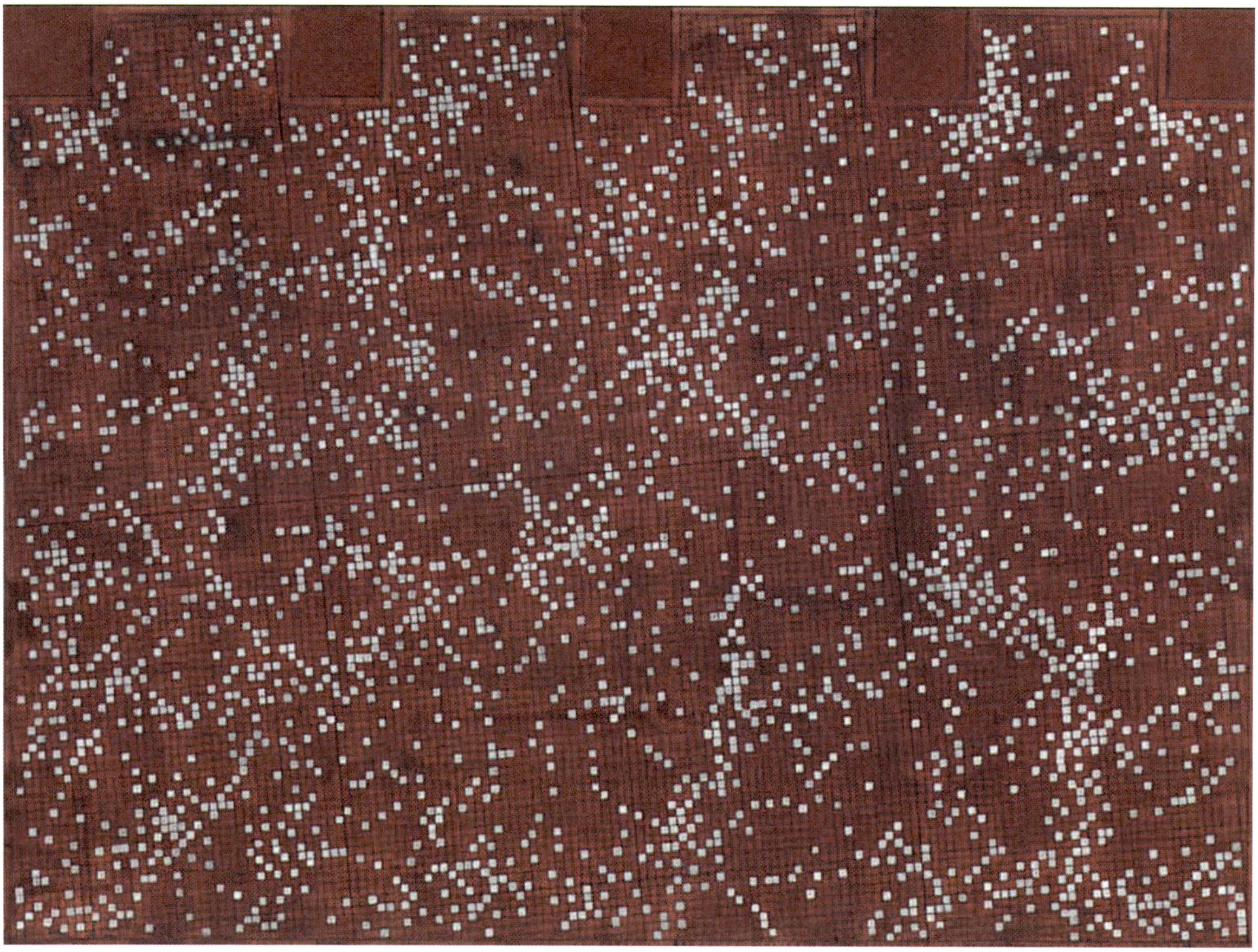

Precedent study colourfield 'Fall', roof (top) and floor (bottom). Paintings by Benoît van Innis

Pragmatic poetry

Marie-José Van Hee in conversation with Colm mac Aoidh

We didn't build our bridges simply to avoid walking on water. Nothing so obvious. A bridge is a meeting place.
    Jeanette Winterson, *The Passion*[1]

While Marie-José Van Hee is best known as an architect of carefully designed and finely crafted houses, many people might be surprised to know that, during the course of the last thirty years or so, she has designed no less than a dozen bridges. The fact that, to date, none of these designs has actually been built has remained a source of disappointment for the architect.

Megalithic bridge in Artannes sur Thouet, France, photographed by Marie-José Van Hee, 2015

Thankfully, this is soon set to change: at the time of writing, two of Van Hee's bridge designs are currently in execution. The first of these is the Verapazbrug in Ghent, in collaboration with Maat-ontwerpers and Witteveen+Bos engineers. An essential piece of city infrastructure, it will ease congestion on the stretched-to-capacity inner ring road by relocating heavy traffic away from the quays, thereby enabling the city to expand outwards in the form of a new residential neighbourhood in the old docklands. The second is an extension – or rather, a continuation – of the renewal project Van Hee has already carried out in collaboration with Robbrecht en Daem architecten in the city of Deinze. This bridge over the River Leie will serve a similar function, connecting a new residential neighbourhood to the city centre and providing a much-needed link for pedestrians and cyclists that highlights the city's shift towards a more sustainable urban mobility.

'It's always been a dream of mine to build a bridge', Van Hee affirms. When discussing her bridges, she often presents an image by French photographer Dominique Issermann. It shows Issermann's niece Anne lying on a concrete wall along the bank of the River Seine while the enormous *Pont de Normandie*, then the longest cable-stayed bridge in the world, soars overhead, eventually disappearing into the mist across the water. 'For me, that photograph is a symbol, a picture that makes visible the dream of making a bridge'.

Van Hee views a bridge as more than a mere object that facilitates the crossing of an obstacle or barrier: 'A bridge is an architectural act that is important for a whole area, because you're linking two places that were not linked before.' She references Gion A. Caminada's *On the Path to Building*, which describes how the building of a bridge gives rise to a place: 'It connects the riverbanks, brings together the paths, the landscape, the people. Thing and place are closely interrelated.'[2]

Caminada emphasises the importance of the relationship between the bridge and its context, and Van Hee's approach to bridge design, much the same as with all of her buildings, is similarly informed by the context. 'I never had the intention to make a bridge somewhere in an open area, where the best solution is a purely technical one that finds the easiest way across from one side to the other. I was always looking for projects that offered the challenge to do something with the landscape, to interact with the surroundings.'

Lynn Geesaman, Parc de Canon, France, 1995

One such project, a collaboration with engineer Dirk Jaspaert, was a competition entry for *Parkbosbruggen*, a pair of pedestrian and cyclist bridges that would connect the centre of Ghent to Parkbos, an area on the outskirts of the city that is being developed into a multifunctional leisure space incorporating parkland and woodland. Transected by three busy arterial routes – the R4 main Ghent ring road, the Ringvaart canal, and the E40 motorway between Oostende and Brussels – this difficult site is neither a natural, rural landscape, nor properly urban, but of rather indeterminate character. The proposed pedestrian and cycle path would partly follow the track of the disused *de Pintelaan* railway line, which previously had run in a relatively straight line from the city to the area of the new park. This legible line in the landscape, still traceable in the straight avenue of trees that had grown along the route of the abandoned railway track, formed for Van Hee the backbone of the site, now severed by the criss-crossing highways and the relatively recently built canal.

 Her idea was to reconnect the dislocated sections of the former railway line with a pair of bridges built in steel that would serve as an extension of the tree-lined avenue. Referencing the form of old railway truss bridges, their load-bearing superstructure and bracing

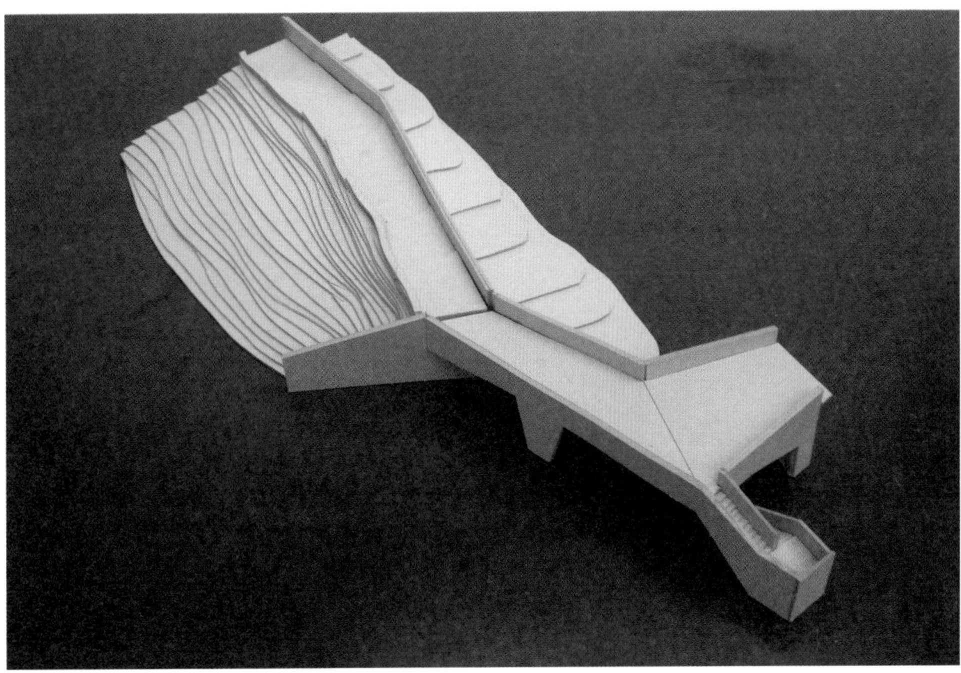

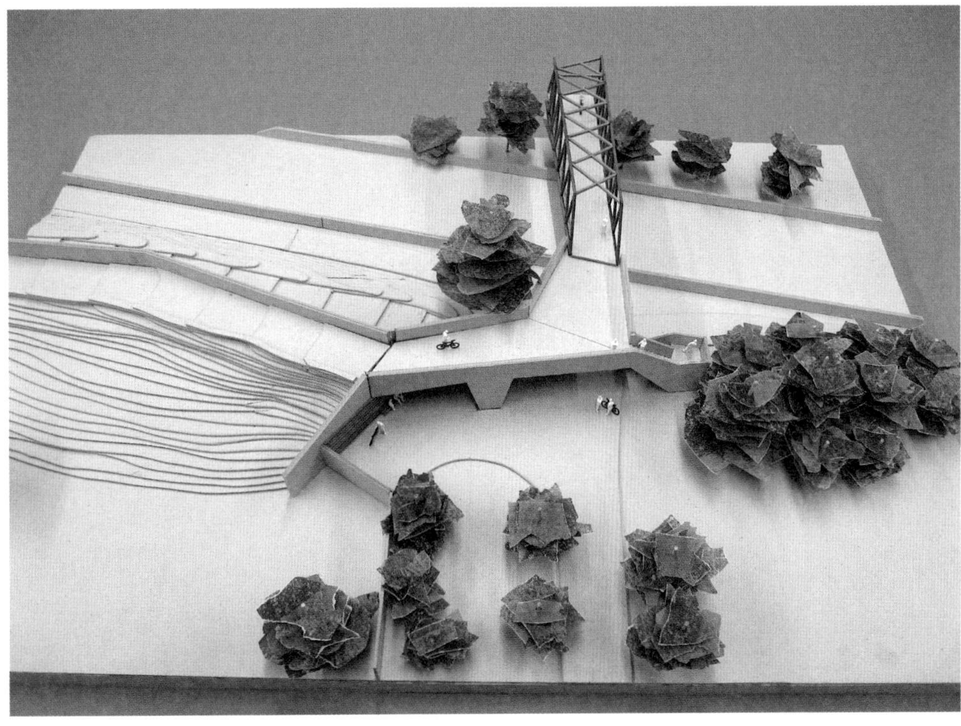

Parkbosbruggen, 2010, unbuilt

Verapazbrug, 2013 – ongoing

would be wrapped around the bridge deck, forming a kind of tunnel that one could walk or cycle through, thereby emphasising and elongating the existing line in the landscape. Van Hee offers an evocative image of the type of linear perspective the proposal would create, in a photograph from Lynn Geesaman of a view through a tree-lined boulevard in *Parc de Canon* in France, where the branches arch overhead, funnelling one's vision towards the horizon.

Since it is an important inland shipping route, the Ringvaart canal had to remain unobstructed for the passage of larger vessels, meaning the bridges needed to be raised at a considerable height. For this reason, large bridgeheads were developed at either end of the bridges, hybrid constructions formed by earth ramparts that would serve as the slopes for bicycle access to the bridge, and a concrete 'dome' construction, incorporating a staircase for pedestrians, with a platform on top and a sheltered undercroft beneath.

These bridgeheads were to form the abutments upon which the steel bridge construction would rest, representing nodes or intersections along the route, their fortress-like appearance making them reference points in the landscape. Van Hee created a meeting place in the underside of this concrete construction, with a bench where people could sit. Integrated lighting provided illumination and improved security at night, the bridgeheads shining as beacons in the landscape, guiding people through the darkness.

Van Hee identifies the troublesome beginning and end points as the most challenging aspects of designing a bridge. 'The most difficult thing, no matter how big a bridge is, is that the foot of the bridge starts from zero, just nothing. What do you do with that? There is a moment when it becomes useful, where you can walk under it, but until that point it's just something to trip over, something you have to make a detour around. It's a block in front of you.'

In the case of Verapazbrug in Ghent, currently in execution, the competition-winning design by Van Hee and Maat-ontwerpers solved this problem quite ingeniously.

The new bridge will connect the two sides of the old docks, from Muidelaan at the North Dock, to Afrikalaan at the South Dock. At the northern end, disused concrete structures known as *grindbakken*, formerly used as silos to hold gravel offloaded from boats, line the waterside. Since the bottom of the empty silos lies a few metres lower than the adjacent road and street level, the proposal took advantage of this height difference to create a passage for pedestrians and cyclists through the grindbakken, providing enough headroom to allow them to pass under the point where the bridge begins to rise over the water.

In order to break up the mass of the bridge, which carries four lanes of motor traffic, two in each direction, the Verapazbrug has in fact been developed as two autonomous constructions, independent of one another and separated by a gap around 4 metres wide. This allows light to penetrate the underside of the bridge, giving a more open quality to the passage underneath.

A small park is created on the southern side, and the concrete stairs at both ends of the bridge that provide a shortcut for pedestrians to descend are each marked by a single tree, planted in the middle of a platform that offers a viewing point looking out over the city.

In each of her housing projects, Van Hee has a habit of planting a tree. This began during her student days: the first thing she did when she moved into a small worker's cottage in Varkensstraat, where two decades later she would build her current home, was plant a tree in the backyard. In part inspired by a need to feel connected with nature, to be rooted to the earth, it is a tradition that consciously harks back to more ancient customs of demarcating space and place, and is a theme that she has carried over to her bridges.

By planting a tree to mark the beginning and end of the bridge, often with a bench at its base, Van Hee is intentionally referencing the Flemish tradition of the planting of a landmark tree. Normally a linden tree, these were planted in the centre of the village, on the main square, at a crossroads, or next to the church. Historically these trees served an important social function as a meeting place – town gatherings would be held under the shelter of its branches, and marriage ceremonies were officiated there. Often living to be centuries old, the height of these trees made them a beacon in the landscape, a reference point and navigational aid that could be seen from far away. Van Hee employs trees in much the same way, to mark the bridge as a meeting place, but also to invite people to read the landscape as a way of orienting themselves. 'What to me is interesting, is to give the bridge something more – it's not only connecting, it's also a meeting place, it's belonging to a landscape, it's belonging to a history.'

Van Hee has worked with the engineer Dirk Jaspaert for most of her bridge designs. 'Everything with Dirk has been an exchange, to allow us to keep moving forward. You must learn to make obstacles your friend, that way you can find new possibilities. If you take into account the essence, as well as material and technical considerations, these implications can help you create something specific. You can make the most necessary thing also a beautiful thing, and it will make your project richer.'

To illustrate her point, Van Hee mentions the Pont Neuf in Toulouse, a 16th century stone bridge which features distinctive round openings in the structural piers. These *dégueuloirs* are a common feature of the ancient Roman bridges that can still be found in the South of France, such as the *Pont Tibère* in Sommières and the *Pont Julien* in Bonnieux. Instead of being merely decorative, in times of flooding they perform an important function, by acting as additional drainage outlets that serve to reduce the hydraulic load on the bridge structure, thereby preventing it from being swept away by the flood waters.

Pont Neuf, Toulouse, 1544

As well as Verapazbrug, the other bridge designed by Van Hee that is currently in execution is a pedestrian and cyclist bridge over the River Leie in Deinze. The continuation of an ongoing redevelopment of the public spaces in the city centre, it will link to the already-completed projects of the Market Square and the renovated river banks of the Leie, which were carried out in collaboration with Robbrecht en Daem architecten. The bridge is a key component of the spatial framework for Deinze that aims to strengthen Martinuspark as a city park and recreation space by improving accessibility and fully integrating it with the city centre.

Because the bridge spans a navigable waterway and therefore has to open to allow boats to pass, it has been designed in consultation with the Flemish Waterways Agency. Working with the engineers from the agency, Van Hee says, has been an informative and productive collaboration. 'They were very interested in how we saw the problem as architects, how to find solutions for opening a bridge, how to find solutions for access to the open bridge. And we were integrating everything they told us. That's the challenge of designing a bridge: it's a piece of infrastructure, it's quite technical with many elements that need to be included.'

How an architect approaches this, she points out, is very different to how an engineer might: 'They tend to just put all the elements together, without having an oversight of their relationship as part of the whole design. For us, as architects, we approached it in the same way you would when you make a public space. You need to integrate a lot of things: benches, lighting, even the rubbish bins, so you have to be very strict about where to put this and where to put that, to be able to organise it as a space, and not just as an ensemble of things. It's more than a sum of all the parts.'

Concrete abutments project out from the riverbanks on either side, supporting a steel bridge deck. This deck is hinged at the Brielpoort side, and can pivot upwards in order to open the Leie to boat traffic. The railing of the balustrade is executed in wood, a motif that is recurrent in many of Van Hee's bridge designs. Formed by two staggered rows of vertical wooden posts, offset by half the horizontal distance between them, the inner row meets the top surface of the bridge deck, while the outer row projects further downwards, so that the bottom of the vertical wooden posts are aligned with the underside of the bridge deck. This partially obscures the steel edge of the deck itself, and gives the impression that the bridge is formed by a horizontal array of floating vertical wooden elements, held in position by an invisible mesh.

Van Hee has also designed a second bridge to further connect Martinuspark to the area bounded by Tolpoortstraat and Gentstraat, which despite being close in proximity to the city centre is very poorly connected.

The shape of this bridge doesn't take the shortest route over the water, but instead continues the existing axis of Bisschopstraat, an elegant solution that absorbs the change of direction as the bridge meets the curve of the path on the opposite side. A side branch off the main bridge axis allows a direct connection to the southern end of the park, giving the bridge a distinctive Y-shape in plan. The area between the two arms of the Y becomes a refuge for wildlife and nature, overgrown with reeds and other water plants.

The wooden railing of the bridge echoes that of the nearby bridge at Brielpoort, with its double row of vertical wooden posts. Here, however, the distortion of perception is more pronounced, since the bottom ends of the outer row of posts do not stop in line with the underside of the bridge, but overhang it, so that they are almost touching the surface of the water. This gives them the appearance of reed stems growing up out of the river, a perception that is further distorted by their reflection on the water's surface. Where the row of posts reaches the riverbanks on the side of the park, similar wooden posts are driven into the ground to continue the balustrade and mark the start and end point of the bridge, heightening the impression that the bridge has grown up out of the reeds.

The joy at finally seeing some of her bridge designs being realised, something Van Hee had dreamt about for so many years, has been tempered somewhat by the disappointment of not being selected to renovate and extend what had been the architect's biggest solo project to date, the ModeNatie building in Antwerp. The usual grief experienced upon losing a competition is in this case amplified by a pain that is felt even more acutely, since no architect likes to think that they will outlive their creations. It is difficult to imagine how it must feel to see one's project, after a series of long and complex negotiations from the initial concept through to the execution phase, finally take shape and become reality, only to watch it, less than two decades later, being extensively altered by another architect with a different vision.

While there is some solace in the fact that the winning design was chosen in part because it promised to respect at least some of Van Hee's original project, leaving the monumental, sculptural staircase and spacious entrance hall untouched, Van Hee fears that other planned changes will cause irrevocable damage to integral features of the building, to the extent that her initial intention will no longer be recognisable.

One of the main goals of the planned renovation is to optimise the museum infrastructure – considerable advances have been made in the technical standards for the preservation of museum artefacts since MoMu first opened in 2002. In order to bring the museum's exhibition and storage spaces up to date, the retrofitting of new systems is necessary. It was suggested in the competition brief for the renovation that these new installations be accommodated inside a new technical zone, to be created by constructing a new partition wall one metre inside the existing one, behind which all the pipes, ducts and other technical paraphernalia could be placed. A suspended false ceiling would incorporate any necessary ceiling installations, with all the surfaces of the galleries completely lined. The overall aim is the creation of an empty space, with flat, uninterrupted walls and ceiling, to provide a neutral backdrop for the exhibits; a tabula rasa which, in theory at least, would be easier to organise and reorganise for each new exhibition.

Baulking at the suggestion of creating a box within a box as a solution for integrating the technical installations, Van Hee is firmly against the idea of designing a hermetic, sterilised gallery space, the archetypal 'white cube' so eloquently dissected by the critic Brian O'Doherty in his famous 1976 essay, *Inside the White Cube*: 'The outside world must not come in, so windows are usually sealed off. Walls are painted white. The ceiling becomes the source of light … The art is free, as the saying used to go, to take on its own life.'[3]
Just like O'Doherty, Van Hee recognises that 'the white wall's apparent neutrality is an illusion.'[4] These blank rooms, while seeming to offer infinite, undifferentiated potentiality, in fact represent a kind of abstract non-space, one that neglects the myriad latent opportunities waiting to be tapped by working within the existing parameters of the space *as found*. 'This is a building with so many possibilities', Van Hee argues, 'why would you just make a white space of it, just nothing?'

By contrast, Van Hee's guiding principle during her original renovation of ModeNatie in 2002 was to engage with the particularity

ModeNatie, competition refurbishment and extension, 2016

top: Bridge over River Leie, 2011 – ongoing
middle and bottom: Bridge Bisschopsstraat Deinze, 2011 – ongoing

and character of what already existed. Through her interventions, she aimed to amplify what was already there, allowing the existing fabric to have an absolute equivalence with the new. Great emphasis was placed on the structural logic of the existing building remaining visible and legible – the beams and columns that can be seen in late 19th and early 20th century photos of the building are still recognisable in the current ModeNatie, albeit sometimes in slightly altered form. Proposing to cover these elements up completely was unthinkable to Van Hee, so unsurprisingly she ignored the suggestion of a box-within-a-box solution. Instead, her competition entry for the 2018 renovation, developed in collaboration with Robbrecht en Daem, proposed to integrate the necessary new technical systems without drastically altering the interior spaces. Speaking about the proposal, which was ultimately rejected by the museum, she admits: 'It's very difficult to kill your own ideas about how to work with a building the way it is. People often seem to have no idea how to work with the history of a building. But when you have such a nice building, why not do something with it?'

She recalls that the Martin Margiela 20th anniversary retrospective was one of the exhibitions at MoMu where the relationship between the objects on display and the space in which they were exhibited was best understood. Margiela and his co-curators created a spatial experience where the interior had a tangible resonance with the exhibition, and vice versa.

'He took photographs of the interior elevation, with the window shutters and the wainscot panelling, behind which we had integrated the pipes and technical installations, and the grilles for the heat and ventilation, done in a fine lattice. So there was in fact a kind of interior façade, with a sense of depth that made a sort of relief. Margiela produced 1:1 scale, life-sized photographs of these elevations, which he hung next to the actual walls, perpendicular to them. So you came into the room and were faced with the real façade and then next to it, the same façade duplicated. And perhaps that was the first time that many people actually noticed this interior façade.'

These large-scale reproductions of interiors represent something of a signature technique for Margiela, who in his boutiques often employed full-size photographs of architectural features such as doorways, staircases and windows as a form of trompe l'oeil, sometimes placing the facsimile right next to the original. Given Margiela's predilection for housing his stores in old buildings, sensitively restored in a manner that strove to respect the architecture and history of the spaces, it is perhaps not surprising that his approach to exhibition design aligns closely with that of Van Hee's architecture, and that the two quite easily complement and accentuate one another.

Van Hee remains characteristically stoic and pragmatic about her experience with ModeNatie, remarking that, 'Of course, every director has their own ideas about running a museum, and a building can always change over time.' As Eugène-Emmanuel Viollet-le-Duc wrote in the 19th century, the architect must learn to finish what others have begun, but also begin what others will finish.

Marie-José Van Hee proved with her renovation of the ModeNatie building in 2002, a project undertaken solely by herself rather than in collaboration with another architect, that she was capable of translating the ideas she had already explored and refined in her housing projects to a larger, urban scale. The projects carried out in collaboration with Robbrecht en Daem architecten, which reorganised and improved public spaces in the city centres of Ghent and Deinze, saw

Van Hee transpose these ideas to an even wider scale and context, and begin to work with landscape elements such as the River Leie.

The bridges that will soon be realised represent a further step in this engagement with the landscape. The closest Van Hee's work has come yet to the discipline of engineering, they can be seen as the logical culmination of her interest in conjugating pragmatism with poetry. At the same time, they continue to adhere to the principle of recognising and exploiting the possibilities inherent in the context that has remained a constant focus throughout her career.

A key inspiration for many of her bridges has been Sint-Michiels-helling in the historical city centre of Ghent. 'I find that a very good bridge, because it does much more than just make the span. It's more than a technical solution. It's a bridge with a façade, it's architectural. It has context, urban context, and from that it makes a place. And that's what I've tried to do with the bridges for Parkbos and Verapaz.'

model Sint-Michielshelling, 1911

Advocating strongly for an architecture that similarly offers more, in every sense, Van Hee insists, 'You can change people's perspective, help them look at things differently by what you do in your architecture. I think architecture should have some complexity, to make it surprising. Otherwise it's just a technical thing, not only structurally but also in people's experience, their perception of it. If there's nothing surprising about it, you will experience it as a neutral thing, an unexciting, uneventful bridge or staircase. But you can make a feast out of it, you can make a beautiful bridge or a beautiful staircase.'

Notes

1 Jeanette Winterson, *The Passion* (London: Bloomsbury Publishing Ltd, 1987) p. 57.
2 Gion A. Caminada, *On the Path to Building: A conversation about architecture with Florian Aicher* (Basel: Birkhauser Verlag GmbH, 2018) p. 88.
3 Brian O'Doherty, *Inside the White Cube: The Ideology of the Gallery Space* (San Francisco: The Lapis Press, 1986) p. 15.
4 Ibid., p. 79.

Brielpoortbrug, Deinze, 2019-2021

Biographies

Dr. JAVIER FERNÁNDEZ CONTRERAS is a Spanish architect, theorist and Head of the Department of Interior Architecture at HEAD – Genève. He studied architecture at the Madrid School of Architecture – ETSAM (Master, 2006; PhD, 2013). His doctoral thesis, *Miralles plan: Thinking and Representation in the Architecture of Enric Miralles,* changed the understanding of Miralles' creativity and ranked finalist in the 10th edition of the arquia/tesis competition. His career combines the professional and academic practices of architecture. Dr. Contreras has taught architectural design at ETSAM in Spain (2007-2012), Xi'an Jiaotong-Liverpool University in China (2013-2014) and the Department of Architecture at ETH Zurich in Switzerland (2016). His professional projects have been published in eight books and included in various exhibitions in Europe and USA. His critical essays on architecture and territory, critical representation, and the design techniques of contemporary architects have been published in numerous magazines and books, including *Massilia Annuaire des Études Corbuséennes, Perspectives in Metropolitan Research, Princeton 306090, CIRCO, Drawing Matter, ZARCH, Arquitectura COAM,* and *RA Revista de Arquitectura.*

CHRISTIAN KIECKENS was a Belgian architect, practising since 1974. In 1981 he won the Godecharle-Prize for Architecture, was selected for the Venice Architecture Biennales in 1985 and 1991, and in 1999 was awarded the Flemish Culture Prize for Architecture. Since 1980 he has taught at various institutes, including Sint-Lucas Ghent, Saint-Luc Liège, the Academies for Architecture in Tilburg, Arnhem and Maastricht, the Technical University Eindhoven, the Architectural Association in London, and the Faculty of Design Sciences at the University of Antwerp.

His teaching concentrates mostly on the translation of words into images, into ideas, and finally into concepts, which has also been the main focus of the reflection on his own work. His professional projects have been widely exhibited, in Gallery S65 in Aalst, Col.legi de Arquitectes in Barcelona, Arc-en-Rêve in Bordeaux and deSingel in Antwerp. Many of his projects and texts have been published internationally, in magazines and monographs such as *Form is one Function too, The Place and the Building, Zoeken Denken Bouwen, from XS to XL, LCTR_CKA_WW,* and the double book *Verwoorden Verbeelden.*

COLM MAC AOIDH is a Brussels-based transdisciplinary practitioner, researcher and writer working across design, communication, architecture and urbanism. He studied Visual Communication Design at TU Dublin, followed by Architecture at London Metropolitan University and KU Leuven Sint-Lucas. He has worked with architecture practices in London and Ghent and collaborated with the team of the Brussels Bouwmeester Maitre Architecte on the Horizon 2020 *Urban Maestro* project, which explored and encouraged innovation in urban design governance. He is currently a PhD researcher at Hasselt University, investigating transdisciplinary practices of adaptive reuse through the collaborative platform *Adapt, Reuse.*

HELEN THOMAS is an architect and writer with a PhD from the University of Essex in Art History and Theory. Attracted to all architecture that diverges from a canon, she has written on Latin American and post-colonial architectural history, architectural drawing, and takes an interest in the way that women practice as architects. Having engaged with institutions as an editor and senior lecturer at the Victoria & Albert Museum, Phaidon Press, the Architectural Association and London Metropolitan University, she now writes and produces books. She also collaborates with Drawing Matter and, with Adam Caruso, continues to edit a series on the limits of modernism: *Rudolf Schwarz and the Monumental Order of Things* (2016) follows *Asnago Vender and the Making of Modern Milan* (2014) and *The Stones of Fernand Pouillon* (2013).

KATRIEN VANDERMARLIERE is an art historian, and was responsible for the architecture programme at deSingel International Arts Campus in Antwerp from 1991 to 2002. She curated more than 70 exhibitions of international and Belgian contemporary architects, planners and landscape designers. She was a member of the editorial board of the Flemish Architecture Yearbook (1992-2000), and director of the Flemish Architecture Institute (2002-2010). In Belgium, she has had a particular influence on the presentation of architecture to a non-professional public. Internationally, she was the commissioner for the Belgian Pavilion at the International Architecture Biennale in Venice and in 2004 received the Golden Lion Award for the best pavilion content.

From 2011 to 2014, Katrien Vandermarliere worked as an independent curator for the Flemish Architecture Institute and deSingel International Arts Campus. Since 2014, she has been director of communications for Ney & Partners engineering consultancy, in addition to her freelance work as a curator and editor. She recently curated the furniture exhibition of Marie-José Van Hee with textiles by Marie Mees and Cathérine Biasino at Maniera in Brussels (2017-2018).

Vandemarliere has been a member of countless architecture competition juries, subvention committees and think tanks for the stimulation of architectural culture in Flanders and abroad.

Photo credits

© Archive Marie-José Van Hee architecten:
13-44, 51, 52, 69, 77, 87, 128, 131, 195-197,
207, 233, 251, 266
© Archive City of Ghent: 262
© Dirk Braeckman: 122-123, Courtesy of
Zeno X Gallery, Antwerp and Thomas
Fischer Galerie, Berlin.
© Kristien Daem: 82 (2), 140 (1), 142-145, 166,
167
© Petra Decouttere: 89 (1), 92, 207, 211
© Lennert Dejonghe: 162
© Viktor Derks: 135 (1), 140 (2), 153-154, 164,
165, 180 (3), 225 (2-5)
© Marc Dubois: 136 (2)
© Filip Dujardin: 100
© Mark De Blieck: 98-99, 101-102 (3)
© Céline De Clercq: 166
© Michael De Lausnay: 180 (4)
© Sam De Vocht: 58 (1), 185, 192, 217
© David Grandorge: cover, 88, 89, 108, 110, 113,
127, 132-133, 136-139, 151-152, 170-171, 184, 186,
198-201, 212 (2-4), 213 (1-2), 215, 221 (1-2, 4-5)
© Javier Fernández Contreras: 221 (3), 228 (1)
© Lynn Geesaman: 252
© Noa Gonzalez: 225 (1)
© Marius Grootveld: 82 (1)
© Michiel Hendryckx: 56, 103, 114, 116, 118-
119, 129, 130, 182, 188, 218 (1-2), 219 (3-4)
© Thomas Hick: 105, 169, 195, 202-203
© Jef Jacobs: 4-5
© Inge Ketelers: backcover
© Lander Loeckx: 210, 212 (1), 213 (3-4), 214
© Peter Lorré: 69, 102 (2), 134, 141, 218 (3-4),
219 (1), 247
© Hugo Maertens & Dominique Provost:
244-246
© Wim Menten: 102 (1)
© Mario Palmieri: 72-73
© Maxime Prananto: 176 (3)
© Frederik Vercruysse: 248-249
© Dietlinde Verhaeghe: 61, 268
© Jan Verlinde: 70-71
© Menno Vanderghote: 253
© Frederik Vanpevenage: 93
© Koen Van Damme: 58 (2)
© Maarten Van den Abeele: 208-209
© Tim Van de Velde: 104, 222
© Crispijn Van Sas: 49, 64, 77-81, 83, 90-91,
146-149, 155-163, 166-169, 172, 176 (1-2), 180
(1-2), 190, 219 (2,5-6), 227, 228 (2-4),
234-239, 263

List of projects
© Archive Marie-José Van Hee architecten:
MCMLXXXII – 03 / MCMXCIV – 05 /
MCMXCIV – 06 / MCMXCV – 01 /
MCMXCVII – 01 / MCMXCVIII – 01 /
MCMXCVIII – 08 / MM – 02 (2) /
MMVI – 03 / MMIV – 05 / MMV-01 /
MMXII – 04 / MMXII – 12 /
MCMLXXXVII – 05 / MCMXCII – 02 /
MCMXCV – 03 / MMII – 01 / MMV – 05 /
MMV – 08 / MMV – 10 / MMXIII – 03 /
MMV – 01 / MMV – 06 / MMVI – 03 /
MMVI – 16 / MMX – 05 / MMXII – 08 /
MMXV – 06 / MMXV – 08MMXV – 11 /
MMXVII – 09 / MMXVIII – 06 /
MMXIX – 01 / MMXII – 09 /
MMXVI – 08 / MMXX – 01 / MMXX – 08 /
MMXXI – 10 / MMXXI – 13
© Jan Baes: MMIX – 12
© Sylvie Cosyns: MMVII – 08 / MMXIV – 05 /
MMXIX – 03
© Kristien Daem: MCMLXXXV – 01 /
MCMLXXXVII – 02 / MCMLXXXVIII – 01 /

MCMLXXXVIII – 03 / MCMLXXXVIII – 05 /
MCMLXXXIX – 01 / MCMXC – 04 /
MCMXCI – 01 / MCMXCIII – 02 (1) /
MCMXCIV – 03 / MCMXCVII – 02 /
MCMXCVII – 03 / MCMXCVIII – 02 /
MCMXCIX – 01 (2003) / MM – 03 /
MMIII – 08 / MCMXCVII – 01
© Mattias Deboutte: MMVI – 11
© Petra Decouttere: MMVII – 05 (2)
© Viktor Derks: MCMXCVI – 02 (3) /
MMV – 02 (2) / MMXII – 05 /
MMXIII – 04 (1) / MMXII – 05 /
MMXIII – 08 / MMXIX – 09
© Michel Devos: MCMXCIX – 02
© Michael De Lausnay: MMIX – 14 (1)
© Sam De Vocht: MCMXCIX – 01 (2009-11) /
MMIII – 09 / MMVI – 05 / MMVII – 11 /
MMVII – 16 / MMXIII – 04 (2) /
MMXV – 03 / MMXVII – 07 / MMXX – 01
© Valerie Doutreluingne: MMVII – 06
© Jean Godecharle: MMVIII – 03
© Dirk Goyens: MMI – 03
© David Grandorge: MCMXC – 01 /
MMIII – 06 (1) / MMIV – 04 /
MMV – 02 (1) / MMVII – 05 (1) /
MMVIII – 07 / MMIX – 02 (2) /
MMIX – 07 / MMIX – 10 / MMX – 02
© Michiel Hendryckx: MCMLXXXIII – 01 /
MCMXC – 02 / MCMXCI – 03 /
MMVIII – 04
© Thomas Hick: MMVII – 03
© Sahar Jaber: MMXII – 04
© Cathérine Libeert: MMXIV – 01
© Daniël Libens: MCMLXXVII – 01 /
MCMLXXVIII – 01 / MCMLXXXVI – 01
© Peter Lorré: MCMXCIX – 01 (2004) /
MM – 02 (1) / MMI – 04 (1)
© Carmen Osten: MMX – 12
© Henk Pijpaert: MMIX – 02 (1)
© Filip Reumers: MMI – 05 / MMII – 05 /
MMIII – 12
© Diego Sanchez: MMXI – 07
© Alice Sanders: MMXIX – 06
© Ellen Smets: MCMXCIV – 05
© Tv Robbrecht en Daem architecten –
Marie-José Van Hee architecten:
MCMXCIX – 01 (2016) / MMIV – 02 /
MMV – 05 / MMXV – 14
© Tv Marie-José Van Hee architecten – José
Maria Sanchez arquitectos: MMXV – 17
© Tv Marie-José Van Hee architecten – Maat
Ontwerpers: MMXII – 04
© Maarten Vanbelle: MMIII – 02
© Marthe Vandenabeele: MMXV – 08
© Menno Vanderghote: MMXI – 09 /
MMXIX – 10
© Frederik Vercruysse: MMIX – 14 (2)
© Dietlinde Verhaeghe: MCMXCIV – 02 /
MMII – 01 /
© Wim Voorspoels: MMIII – 04
© Tim Van de Velde: MCMXCVI – 02 (1-2)
© Crispijn Van Sas: MCMLXXIX – 02 /
MCMXCI – 04 / MMI – 04 (2) /
MMIII – 05 / MMVII – 14 / MMVII – 15 /
MMVII – 02 / MMX – 01 / MMXIV – 03 /
MCMLXXVII – 01 / MCMLXXXVII – 01 /
MCMXC – 01 / MCMXCI – 01 /
MCMXCIII – 02 (2) / MCMXCVII – 01 (1) /
MMIII – 06 (2) / MMIII – 11 / MMIV – 01 /
MMIX – 11 / MMX – 11 / MMX – 08 /
MMX – 15 / MMXI – 05 / MMXII – 05 /
MMXII – 06 / MMXIV – 02 / MMXIV – 06 /
MMXV – 04 / MMXV – 12 / MMXVII – 09 /
MMXVIII – 03 / MMXIX – 01 /
© Peter Van Tornhout: MMVII – 12

Colophon

Content and concept 2019: Marie-José Van Hee, Viktor Derks, Lennert Dejonghe, Sam De Vocht
Second revised edition 2025: Marie-José Van Hee, Sam De Vocht
Translation Dutch to English: Gregory Ball, Sam De Vocht, Colm mac Aoidh
Translation English to French: Alain Kinsella, Brussels
Translation English to German: Miriam Seifert-Waibel, Hamburg
Proofreading: Marie-José Van Hee, Viktor Derks, Sam De Vocht, Lisa Franke, Jérôme Kockerols, Colm mac Aoidh, Brigid Margaret Magee, Susanne Pietsch, Frédéric Timmermans
Image selection: Marie-José Van Hee, Viktor Derks, Lennert Dejonghe, Sam De Vocht, Inge Ketelers
Plans and drawings: Viktor Derks, Céline De Clercq, Uršula Novak, Maaike Snel
Illumination of maps: Vinciane Lowie
Graphic design: Inge Ketelers
Typefaces: William Text (Maria Doreuli), Union (Radim Peško)
Printing and binding: Printer Trento S.R.L., Trento

Many thanks to our clients, the artists, authors and photographers for their contributions to this publication.

Special thanks to the Flanders Architecture Institute and De Singel, CIVA, Abe Bonnema-stichting, Beeldbank Gent and Archipel vzw.
Thank you, Inge, for making this beautiful book. Thank you Linus at Quart Verlag for your confidence and support.
Marie-José Van Hee would like to thank collaborators, family & friends, Vinciane Lowie & Peter Derks, Marleen Theunis, Michel Devos, Peter Vanooteghem and many more for their continuing support over the years.

MJVHa would like to express their gratitude to the following persons, whose generous support made this book possible in 2019: Bouwmeester Declercq, Nevele; Anonymous, Ghent; Atelier Provost, Beernem; ADW schrijnwerk, Lokeren; Bailleul Ontwerpbureau, Ghent; Florian Beigel & Philip Christou, London; Rinaldo Castelli, Wortegem-Petegem; Els Claessens & Kristiaan Borret, Brussels; Marjan Coppens & Johan Van Hee, Deinze; Apotheek De Causmaecker, Lokeren; Landschapsatelier Arne Deruyter, Machelen-aan-de-Leie – Stad Deinze; Isabelle De Bruyn & Ignace Vandenabeele, Ghent; Sam De Vocht & Juan Duque, Brussels; HdF, Zuidzande; Eggermont natuursteen bvba, Deinze; Javier Fernández Contreras, Granada; Bart Gielen, Gielen Building, Ghent; Kathleen Gunst & Tom Degryse, Torhout; Niall Hobhouse, Somerset; David Kohn, London; Barbara Marie-Reine & Daniel Rosbottom, London; OCMW Deinze; Stefan Paeleman, Oudergem; Robbrecht en Daem architecten, Ghent; Seghers Landschapsarchitecten, Zottegem; Stone NV, Olsene; Wim Supply, Brugge; Universiteitsbibliotheek, Ghent; Machteld Van den Abeele, Ghent; Ellen Van Hee & Bart Muskala, Bachte-Maria-Leerne; Kathleen Wijnant & Jonas Van Hee, Bachte-Maria-Leerne

Second, revised edition, originally published in 2019 by Slow Publishing, Ghent

© 2025 Marie-José Van Hee architecten and Quart Verlag GmbH
© for the images: see photo credits
© for the texts: the authors

Product safety
Responsible person pursuant to EU Regulation 2023/988 (GPSR):
GVA Gemeinsame Verlagsauslieferung Göttingen GmbH & Co. KG
Post Box 2021
37010 Göttingen
Germany
T +49 551 384 200 0
info@gva-verlage.de

Quart Verlag GmbH
Denkmalstrasse 2, CH-6006 Luzern
books@quart.ch, T +41 41 420 20 82
www.quart.ch

ISBN 978-3-03761-315-3 (Booklet French translation)
ISBN 978-3-03761-310-8 (Booklet German translation)

MCMLXXVII – 01
House Valère Van Hee
Bachte-Maria-Leerne
1977-1979 (demolished)

MCMLXXVIII – 01
House Bruinjé
Wachtebeke
1978-1979

MCMLXXIX – 02
House De Blaere – Verstuyft
Maldegem
1979-1981

MCMLXXXII – 03
Distribution transformer
Ghent
1982-1984
with Ignace Bevernage

2018 Protected monument

MCMLXXXIII – 01
House Lowie – Derks
Ghent
1983-1986

2018 Protected monument

MCMLXXXV – 01
Reconversion House Vinken – Van Hee
Passendale
1985-1990
with Johan Van Dessel
with the assistance of Ariane Van Craen

MCMLXXXVI – 01

Shop Comme des Garçons

Brussels
1986-1988
with Johan Van Dessel
with the assistance of Frederic Hossey

MCMLXXXVII – 02

Bank branch office and apartment BACOB

Ukkel, Brussels
1987-1989
with Johan Van Dessel
with Gérard Bolly
with the assistance of Ariane Van Craen

Exhibition
Jonge architecten in België. Museum voor
Sierkunsten, Ghent (BE), Rotterdamse
Kunststichting, Rotterdam (NL) 1986-1987

MCMLXXXVII – 05

Reconversion park pavilion Vauxhall

Brussel
1987-1988
with Johan Van Dessel
with the assistance of Frederic Hossey

MCMLXXXVII – 08

Bank branch office BACOB

Wavre
1987-1989 (demolished)
with Johan Van Dessel
with Gérard Bolly
with the assistance of Dominique Plantefève

MCMLXXXVIII – 01

House, showroom and storage Pay

Laken, Brussels
1988-1991
with Johan Van Dessel
with Gérard Bolly
with the assistance of Ariane Van Craen

2016 Protected monument

MCMLXXXVIII – 03

Reconversion house and office Claeys

Ghent
1988-1990
with Johan Van Dessel
with the assistance of Ariane Van Craen

MCMLXXXVIII – 05

Office and apartments La Source

Sint-Gillis, Brussels
1988-1991
with Johan Van Dessel
with L.M. Chapeaux
with the assistance of Ariane Van Craen

MCMXC – 01

House, office and storehouse Van Hee – Coppens

Deinze
1990-1993
with BAS Dirk Jaspaert, Paul Deroose landscape architect
with the assistance of Els Claessens

MCMXC – 04

Gallery and apartment Hufkens

Elsene, Brussels
1990-1992
with Paul Robbrecht, Hilde Daem
with BAS Dirk Jaspaert
with the assistance of Brigitte D'Hoore

MCMXCI – 01

House Braet – De Paepe

Ghent
1991-1993
with BAS Dirk Jaspaert
with the assistance of Els Claessens

MCMXCI – 03

Pharmacy and House Van Backlé – De Feu

Wemmel
1991-1993
with BAS Dirk Jaspaert
with the assistance of Els Claessens

Exhibition
Architetti della Fiandra. 5. Mostra Internazionale
di Architettura, Belgian Pavilion, Venice (IT)
1991
with Robbrecht en Daem architecten, Christian
Kieckens, Xaveer De Geyter, Paul Vermeulen
and Henk De Smet, Stéphane Beel

MCMXCI – 04

Reconversion house Ouvry
Ghent
1991

2008-2009
Roof apartment
with the assistance of Valerie Doutreluingne

MCMXCII – 02

Social housing Hollainkazerne
Ghent
1992-1993
competition design, unbuilt
with Robbrecht en Daem architecten
with the assistance of Els Claessens, Wim Cuyvers,
Frank De Baere, Sofie Delaere, Brigitte D'Hoore,
Ilse Popelier, Hugo Vanneste

Exhibition
Architetti della Fiandra. 5. Mostra Internazionale
di Architettura, Belgian Pavilion, Venice (IT)
1991
with Robbrecht en Daem architecten, Christian
Kieckens, Xaveer De Geyter, Paul Vermeulen
and Henk De Smet, Stéphane Beel

© Ivan Adriaens

<u>Exhibition</u>
M.-José Van Hee, ontwerpen 1977-1993.
Kunstcentrum deSingel, Antwerp (BE) 1993

<u>Furniture</u>
lectern
Ghent
1993

MCMXCIII – 02
House and pharmacy De Causmaecker – Bouckaert
Lokeren
1993-1995
with Robbrecht en Daem architecten
with BAS Dirk Jaspaert
with the assistance of Sofie Delaere

2014-2020
with the assistance of Jan Baes

MCMXCIV – 01
House Van Hee
Ghent
1994-1997
with BAS Dirk Jaspaert
with the assistance of Els Claessens,
Tania Vandenbussche

© Peter Derks

© Viktor Derks

MCMXCIV – 02

Reconversion House Burssens – Ballegeer

Ghent
1994-1996
with BAS Dirk Jaspaert
with the assistance of Tania Vandenbussche

2003
Doctor's practice

MCMXCIV – 03

Office building Coppens

Roeselare
1994-1996
with the assistance of Tania Vandenbussche
with Jan Leye

MCMXCIV – 05

Reconversion House Geerts – Lambert

Veltem-Beisem
1994-2003
with the assistance of Filip Reumers,
Tania Vandenbussche, Wim Voorspoels

2012-2013
Refurbishment of a bathroom
with the assistance of Sam De Vocht

MCMXCIV – 06

Reconversion House De Tremerie – Van Pevenage

Ghent
1994-1997
with the assistance of Els Claessens,
Tania Vandenbussche

MCMXCV – 01

Reconversion House Vandenbussche

Ghent
1995-1997
with the assistance of Els Claessens,
Tania Vandenbussche

MCMXCV – 03

Housing and apartments Prins Albertkazerne

Brussels
1995
competition design, unbuilt
with Robbrecht en Daem architecten,
Dirk Van de Kerckhove landscape architect
with the assistance of Els Claessens,
Frank De Baere, Sofie Delaere, Brigitte D'Hoore,
Tania Vandenbussche, Hugo Vanneste

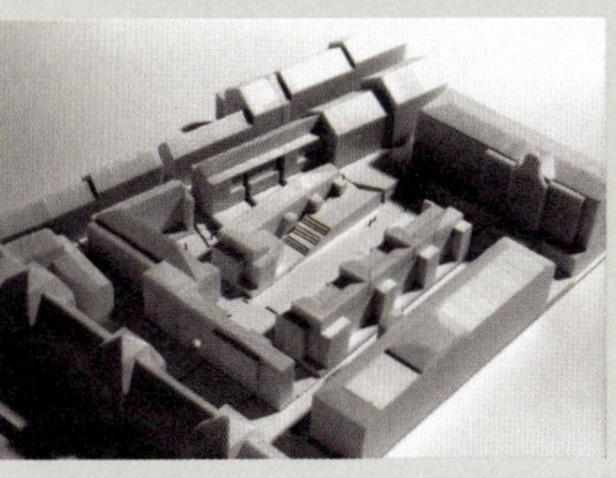

MCMXCVI – 02

Refurbishment of the inner city central
squares Korenmarkt,
Emile Braunplein and Market Hall

Ghent
1996-2012
competition design, laureate
with Robbrecht en Daem architecten, BAS Dirk
Jaspaert, Wirtz International, Technum
with the assistance of Wim Menten, Bert Callens,
Jan Baes, Tom Broes, Katrien Cammers,
Axel Clissen, Mattias Deboutte, Petra Decouttere,
Arne Deruyter, Linde Everaerd, Trice Hofkens,
Gert Jansseune, Daniël Libens, Carmen Osten,
Filip Reumers, Sofie Reynaert, Miriam Rohde,
Johannes Robbrecht, Marilù Sicoli, Gert Swolfs,
Pieter Vanderhoydonck, Kathy Vermeeren,
Caroline Voet, Wim Walschap

Exhibition
De rijkdom van de eenvoud. Fondation pour
l'architecture, Brussels (BE) 1996
Exhibition design with Koen Van Synghel,
Francis Strauven

Exhibition
Nouvelle architecture en Flandre. arc en rêve
centre d'architecture, Bordeaux (FR) 1996

Exhibition
Arquitectura de Flandes. Collegi D'Arquitectes
de Catalunya, Barcelona (ES) 1997

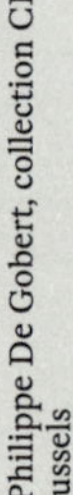
© Philippe De Gobert, collection CIVA, Brussels

© Ivan Adriaens

MCMXCVI – 03
Reconversion House Decru – Logghe

Rumbeke
1996-1999
with Jan Leye
with the assistance of Filip Reumers,
Tania Vandenbussche

MCMXCVII – 01
House L – C

Ghent
1997-2000
with BAS Dirk Jaspaert
with the assistance of Filip Reumers

<u>Furniture</u>

bed-bank

Ghent
1997 (prototype with Peter Van Tornhout) –
2017 (with Frank Ternier)
with the assistance of Sam De Vocht,
Lennert Dejonghe

© Maxime Prananto 2017

MCMXCVII – 03

Refurbishment of Leopold De Waelplaats
Square and surroundings of the Museum
of Fine Arts with 'Deep Fountain' by
Cristina Iglesias
Antwerp
1997-1999
competition design, laureate
with Robbrecht en Daem architecten,
BAS Dirk Jaspaert
with the assistance of Frank De Baere,
Els Claessens, Brigitte D'Hoore, Catherine Fierens,
Shin Hagiwara, Filip Reumers, Tania Vandenbussche

MCMXCVIII – 01

Reconversion House Van Kerckhove –
Dewaele
Ghent
1998-1999
with the assistance of Filip Reumers

MCMXCVII – 02

Reconversion House and Shop
Oosterlinck – Mertens
Wetteren
1997-1999
with BAS Dirk Jaspaert
with the assistance of Filip Reumers,
Tania Vandenbussche

MCMXCVIII – 08

Restoration and reconversion of a former
bank office – Bank van de Arbeid
Ghent
1998, unbuilt
with Ferdinand Schlich
with the assistance of Els Claessens,
Shin Hagiwara, Filip Reumers, Dietlinde Verhaeghe

MCMXCIX – 01

Reconversion 19th century building to
Fashion Museum – ModeNatie
Antwerp
1999-2003
with Bureau Bouwtechniek, BAS Dirk Jaspaert
with the assistance of Leslie Burm, Dirk Goyens,
Shin Hagiwara, Filip Reumers, Johan Suykens,
Tania Vandenbussche, Rolf Vansteenwegen,
Dietlinde Verhaeghe, Wim Voorspoels

2009-2011
Reception desk
with the assistance of Frederik De Smedt,
Sam De Vocht

2016
Competition refurbishment and extension –
not selected
with Robbrecht en Daem, BAS bvba,
Bureau Bouwtechniek
with the assistance of Viktor Derks

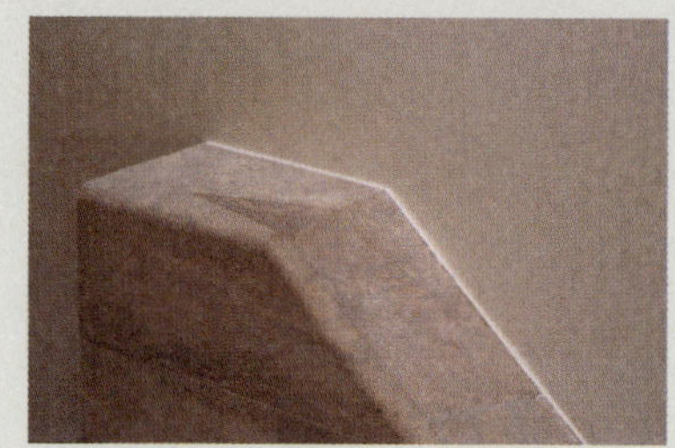

2003

2004

2009-2011

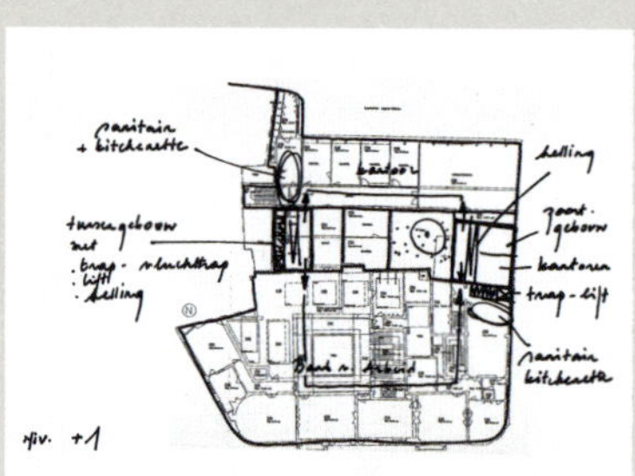

2016

MCMXCIX – 02

Reconversion House Devos

Heusden
1999-2002
with BAS Dirk Jaspaert
with the assistance of Filip Reumers, Dietlinde Verhaeghe

MM – 02

Reconversion House Steel

Ghent
2000-2003
with BAS Dirk Jaspaert
with the assistance of Dietlinde Verhaeghe

MM – 03

Reconversion House Dekeersmaecker – Tollebeek

Sint-Amands
2000-2002
with BAS Dirk Jaspaert
with the assistance of Dirk Goyens

MMI – 03

House Verstraete – Vandewalle

Rumbeke
2001-2003
with BAS Dirk Jaspaert
with the assistance of Dirk Goyens

MMI – 04

House Van Leemput – Oosterlinck

Wetteren
2000-2003
with BAS Dirk Jaspaert
with the assistance of Filip Reumers,
Dietlinde Verhaeghe

MMI – 05

Reconversion House Louis – Manigart

De Pinte
2001-2005
with BAS Dirk Jaspaert
with the assistance of Filip Reumers

Exhibition
One-hundred houses for one-hundred European architects of the XX Century. Kunstencentrum deSingel, Antwerp (BE) 2001

MMII – 01

Housing Schaafstraat

Antwerp
2002, unbuilt
competition design
with BAS Dirk Jaspaert
with the assistance of Rebecca Devriese,
Dirk Goyens, Filip Reumers, Tomas Vandergucht,
Wim Voorspoels, Douwe Wieërs

MMII – 05

Reconversion House and stables
Claes – Dobbelaere

Dikkelvenne
2002-2005
with BAS Dirk Jaspaert
with the assistance of Filip Reumers

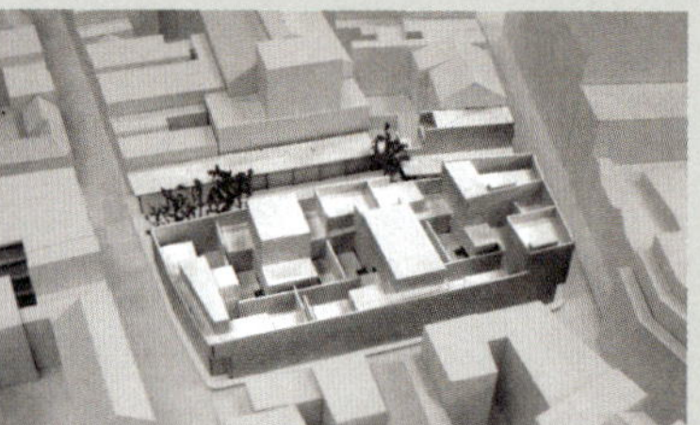

MMII – 01

Passenger Ferry
Ostend and Nieuwpoort
2002, unbuilt
competition design, Open Call 03 by the Flanders
Government Architect
with BAS Dirk Jaspaert, with Jan Kempenaers
and Kris Martin
with the assistance of Dirk Goyens,
Dietlinde Verhaeghe, Wim Voorspoels

MMV – 08

Extension of the City Administration
Offices Bethaniënhuis
Zoersel
2003, unbuilt
competition design, Open Call 03 by the Flanders
Government Architect
with BAS Dirk Jaspaert, Kris Martin
with the assistance of Dirk Goyens,
Dietlinde Verhaeghe, Wim Voorspoels

MMIII – 02

House Janssens – Oosterlinck
Wetteren
2003-2007
with BAS Dirk Jaspaert
with the assistance of Maarten Vanbelle

MMIII – 04

House Berlamont – Degryse
Torhout
2003-2009
with BAS Dirk Jaspaert
with the assistance of Wim Voorspoels

2009 landscaping
with the assistance of Carmen Osten

MMIII – 05

Reconversion House De Borger –
De Brabanter
Rendeux
2003-2005
with BAS Dirk Jaspaert
with the assistance of Dietlinde Verhaeghe

2015 unbuilt
with the assistance of Indra Janda, Jessica
Langerock

MMIII – 06

Office and apartment Bailleul
Ghent
2003-2010
with the assistance of Dietlinde Verhaeghe,
Jan Baes

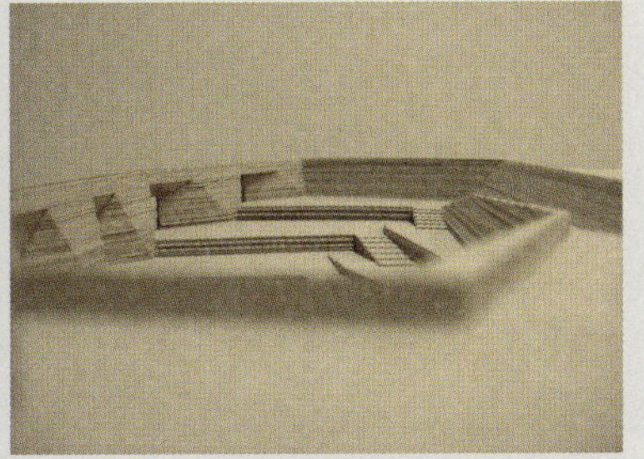

MMIII – 08

House Sierens – Debouck

Ghent
2002-2004
with BAS Dirk Jaspaert
with the assistance of Dirk Goyens

MMIII – 09

House Niemegeerts – Taerwe

Scheldewindeke
2003-2009
with BAS Dirk Jaspaert
with the assistance of Sam De Vocht, Filip Reumers

MMIII – 10

Reconversion House Van Assche – Tomei

Ghent
2003-2006
with BAS Dirk Jaspaert
with the assistance of Tinne Verwerft

MMIII – 11

House Anné – Buyl

Lampernisse
2003-2007
with BAS Dirk Jaspaert, Vandendries Capoen architecten
with the assistance of Wim Voorspoels

MMIII – 12

Reconversion House Camerlinckx – Rans

Heverlee
2003-2005
with BAS Dirk Jaspaert
with the assistance of Filip Reumers

MMIII – 18

City Hall Square

Zoersel
2003, unbuilt
competition design
with Bureau Bouwtechniek, BAS Dirk Jaspaert, with Kris Martin
with the assistance of Maarten Vanbelle, Peter Vanooteghem, Tinne Verwerft

MMIV – 01

Reconversion of a warehouse into
Arts Centre Expeditie

Ghent
2004-2013
with Bureau Bouwtechniek, BAS Dirk Jaspaert,
Henk Pijpaert engineering
with the assistance of Sam De Vocht,
Tinne Verwerft

MMIV – 02

Refurbishment of inner city central
squares Fochplein and Margarethaplein

Leuven
2004, unbuilt
competition design
with Robbrecht en Daem architecten,
BAS Dirk Jaspaert

MMIV – 04

Reconversion House Vandekerckhove –
Vandeputte

Mariakerke
2004-2005
with BAS Dirk Jaspaert
with the assistance of Dietlinde Verhaeghe,
Wim Voorspoels

MMIV – 05

Private library Bruloot – Michiels

Antwerp
2004-2005
with the assistance of Dietlinde Verhaeghe

MMV – 01

Housing De Wannemaecker

Zottegem
2005-2009, unbuilt
with the assistance of Dietlinde Verhaeghe,
Tinne Verwerft, Wim Voorspoels

MMV – 03

Sound Barrier A12

Meise
2005, unbuilt
competition design, Open Call by the Flanders
Government Architect
with BAS Dirk Jaspaert, Paul Deroose
with the assistance of Maarten Vanbelle,
Dietlinde Verhaeghe, Tinne Verwerft,
Wim Voorspoels

MMV – 05

Refurbishment of the city boulevard Rooseveltplaats in front of the Opera House

Antwerp
2005, unbuilt
competition design, Open Call by the Flanders Government Architect
with Robbrecht en Daem architecten, Wirtz International, Sum Research
with the assistance of Kristoffel Boghaert, Katrien Cammers, Suzanne Desmet, Bert Haerynck, Charlotte Pattyn, Maarten Vanbelle, Liesbet Vandenbussche, Dietlinde Verhaeghe, Wim Voorspoels, Wouter Willems

MMV – 06

Koninklijke Baan Pedestrian Bridge

Wenduine
2005, unbuilt
competition design, Open Call by the Flanders Government Architect
with BAS Dirk Jaspaert
with the assistance of Maarten Vanbelle, Pieter Vansteeger, Dietlinde Verhaeghe, Wim Voorspoels

MMV – 10

Masterplan 'Le Grand Large'

Dunkerque (FR)
2005, unbuilt
competition design
with Robbrecht en Daem architecten

MMV – 12

Crematorium

Kortrijk
2005, unbuilt
competition design, Open Call 09 by the Flanders Government Architect
with Bureau Bouwtechniek, Paul Deroose, Peter Vanooteghem
with the assistance of Maarten Vanbelle, Pieter Vansteeger, Dietlinde Verhaeghe, Tinne Verwerft, Wim Voorspoels

MMV – 02

House and doctor's practice Van Aelten – Oosterlinck

Opwijk
2005-2011
with BAS Dirk Jaspaert, Seghers landschapsarchitecten
with the assistance of Mattias Deboutte, Dietlinde Verhaeghe, Wim Voorspoels

2014-2016 swimming pond and pool house
with the assistance of Viktor Derks

MMVI – 03

Housing Nieuwstraat

Kortrijk
2006, unbuilt
with Bureau Bouwtechniek, BAS Dirk Jaspaert
with the assistance of Maarten Vanbelle, Tinne Verwerft

MMVI – 05
Extension House Clinckspoor
Wichelen
2006-2007
with BAS Dirk Jaspaert
with the assistance of Sam De Vocht,
Peter Vanooteghem

MMVI – 11
Reconversion House Demeester
Ghent
2006-2009
with BAS Dirk Jaspaert
with the assistance of Mattias Deboutte,
Tinne Verwerft

MMVI – 16
Zennegat cyclist bridges
Mechelen
2006, unbuilt
competition design, Open Call 11 by the Flanders
Government Architect
with BAS Dirk Jaspaert, Bureau Bouwtechniek
with the assistance of Sam De Vocht, Maarten
Vanbelle, Dietlinde Verhaeghe, Wim Voorspoels

MMVII – 03
House HdF
Zuidzande (NL)
2007-2011
with BAS Dirk Jaspaert, Henk Pijpaert engineering,
Aldrik Heirman landscape architect
with the assistance of Sam De Vocht,
Mattias Deboutte, Wim Voorspoels

MMVII – 05
House and studio Vandewalle – Van Damme
Ghent
2007-2013
with BAS Dirk Jaspaert
with the assistance of Sam De Vocht

MMVII – 06
House Bracke
Wetteren
2007-2012
with BAS Dirk Jaspaert
with the assistance of Sam De Vocht,
Valerie Doutreluingne

MMVII – 08

Reconversion House Verstraete – Compernolle

Sint-Denijs-Westrem
2007-2012
with BAS Dirk Jaspaert, Wirtz International
with the assistance of Sam De Vocht, Valerie
Doutreluingne

2014-2019 carport and pool house
with the assistance of Sylvie Cosyns, Sam De Vocht

MMVII – 11

Reconversion House Derks – Lowie

Mariakerke
2007-2010
with the assistance of Jan Baes
Reconversion of a house by René Heyvaert

MMVII – 12

Reconversion House Van Tornhout

Landegem
2007-2009
with BAS Dirk Jaspaert
with the assistance of Peter Vanooteghem

MMVII – 14

House Muskala – Van Hee

Bachte-Maria-Leerne
2007-2010
with BAS Dirk Jaspaert
with the assistance of Frederik De Smedt,
Valerie Doutreluingne

2019 – ongoing, studio
with the assistance of Jessica Langerock

MMVII – 15

House V-D

Ghent
2007-2019
with BAS Dirk Jaspaert, Henk Pijpaert engineering,
Ludovic Devriendt landscape architect
with the assistance of Jan Baes, Lennert Dejonghe

MMVII – 16

House Marchal

Ghent
2007-2011
with the assistance of Mattias Deboutte

MMVIII – 02

House and dental practice Degryse – Gunst

Torhout
2008-2013
with BAS Dirk Jaspaert, burO Groen
with the assistance of Sam De Vocht,
Valerie Doutreluingne

2015-ongoing, new entrance with staircase and lift
with the assistance of Sylvie Cosyns,
Wannes De Brouwer, Sam De Vocht, Uršula Novak,
Ben Rea

MMVIII – 03

House De Baets – Jooris

Ghent
2008-2010
with the assistance of Indra Janda, Tinne Verwerft

MMVIII – 04

Reconversion Family House Van Hee

Le Puy-Notre-Dame, Maine-et-Loire (FR)
2008-2022
with BAS Dirk Jaspaert
with the assistance of Jan Baes, Mattias Deboutte,
Lennert Dejonghe, Viktor Derks, Thomas Faes,
Menno Vanderghote

MMVIII – 07

Reconversion showroom and House Lambers – Decru

Ghent
2008-2012
with BAS Dirk Jaspaert
with the assistance of Carmen Osten

MMIX – 02

House Pijpaert – Aers

Oudenaarde
2009-2014
with BAS Dirk Jaspaert
with the assistance of Indra Janda,
Jessica Langerock

MMIX – 07

Reconversion House Braeckman – De Rijcke

Gavere
2009-2014
with BAS Dirk Jaspaert
with the assistance of Mattias Deboutte,
Indra Janda, Jessica Langerock

MMIX – 10
Reconversion House Kongs
Ghent
2009-2016
with BAS Dirk Jaspaert
with the assistance of Sam De Vocht,
Carmen Osten

2020-2022
with the assistance of Alice Sanders

MMIX – 11
House and apartments Van Gysel – Strijkers
Kallo
2009-2016
with BAS Dirk Jaspaert
with the assistance of Menno Vanderghote

2018-2021, furniture
with the assistance of Lennert Dejonghe,
Menno Vanderghote

MMIX – 12
Reconversion House Mareel – Costers
Ghent
2009-2011
with BAS Dirk Jaspaert
with the assistance of Jan Baes,
Peter Vanooteghem, Tinne Verwerft

MMIX – 14
Refurbishment of the Market Square, road infrastructure, Reinbachplein, public space and Leie riverbanks
Deinze
2009 – ongoing
competition design, laureate
with Robbrecht en Daem architecten, Engitop
with the assistance of Valerie De Ketelaere,
Jessica Langerock, Carmen Osten, Diego Sanchez,
Kobe Van Praet

MMX – 01
House Coppens – Cocquyt
Landegem
2010-2015
with BAS Dirk Jaspaert
with the assistance of Menno Vanderghote

2017-2019 carport
with the assistance of Sylvie Cosyns

MMX – 02
Reconversion House Leroux – Van Der Hauwaert
Ghent
2010-2015
with BAS Dirk Jaspaert
with the assistance of Sam De Vocht
Reconversion of a house by Paul Felix

MMX – 05

Parkbos pedestrian and cyclist bridges

Ghent
2010, unbuilt
competition design, Open Call 19 by the Flanders
Government Architect
with BAS Dirk Jaspaert
with the assistance of Jan Baes, Mattias Deboutte,
Sam De Vocht, Valerie Doutreluingne,
Yza Hunzinger, Carmen Osten, Menno Vanderghote

MMX – 08

Reconversion House Willems – Van Gils

Ravels
2010-2019
with BAS Dirk Jaspaert
with the assistance of Jan Baes

MMX – 11

Reconversion house into studio
appartments Vandenabeele / 10+11

Ghent
2010-2022
with Studiebureau Tecclem
with the assistance of Sam De Vocht, Jessica
Langerock, Menno Vanderghote

MMX – 12

Reconversion House Van Poele –
Van Thielen

Ghent
2010-2012
with BAS Dirk Jaspaert
with the assistance of Carmen Osten

MMX – 15

Bridge Brielpoortbrug

Deinze
design 2010
construction 2019-2021
with Peter Coppens, City of Deinze, Vlaamse
Waterweg
with the assistance of Céline De Clercq, Jessica
Langerock

MMXI – 05

House Van Hee – Vinken

Passendale
2011-2017
with the assistance of Indra Janda

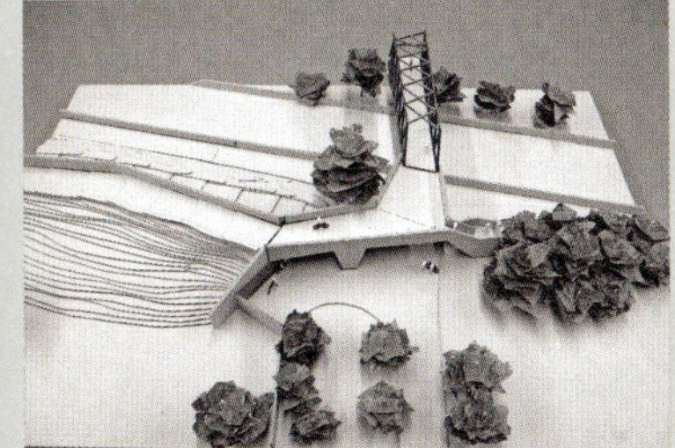

<u>Furniture</u>

huis-werk-tafel

Ghent
2011 – ongoing
2013 – ongoing (with Frank Ternier)
with the assistance of Lennert Dejonghe,
Sam De Vocht, Sahar Jaber

MMXI – 07

House M – V

Sint-Martens-Latem
2011-2013, unbuilt
with BAS Dirk Jaspaert
with the assistance of Sam De Vocht,
Diego Sanchez

MMXI – 09

Stonemason's workshop Eggermont

Haaltert
2011, unbuilt
with BAS Dirk Jaspaert
with the assistance of Menno Vanderghote

© Filip Dujardin

© Crispijn Van Sas

MMXI – 14

Workshop for the Green Maintenance Service, Bredastraat

Antwerp
2011, unbuilt
competition design
with BAS Dirk Jaspaert, Bureau Bouwtechniek, HPe
with the assistance of Jan Baes, Sam De Vocht, Valerie Doutreluingne, Sahar Jaber, Indra Janda, Jessica Langerock, Carmen Osten, Menno Vanderghote

MMXII – 04

Refurbishment and flood control improvement of the seawall

Blankenberge
2012-2019
competition design, laureate
with Maat ontwerpers, Witteveen + Bos
with the assistance of Valerie De Ketelaere, Jessica Langerock, Carmen Osten

MMXII – 05

Reconversion House Verbeke

Ghent
2012-2017
with the assistance of Viktor Derks

MMXII – 08

Refurbishment Town Square

Nazareth
2012, unbuilt
Competition design, Open Call 24 by the Flanders Government Architect
with BAS Dirk Jaspaert
with the assistance of Jan Baes, Sam De Vocht, Valerie Doutreluingne, Indra Janda, Jessica Langerock, Carmen Osten, Menno Vanderghote

MMXII – 09

Landscaping for a Crematorium

Aalst
2012, unbuilt
competition design
with Tony Fretton architects
with the assistance of Tom Appels, Sam De Vocht

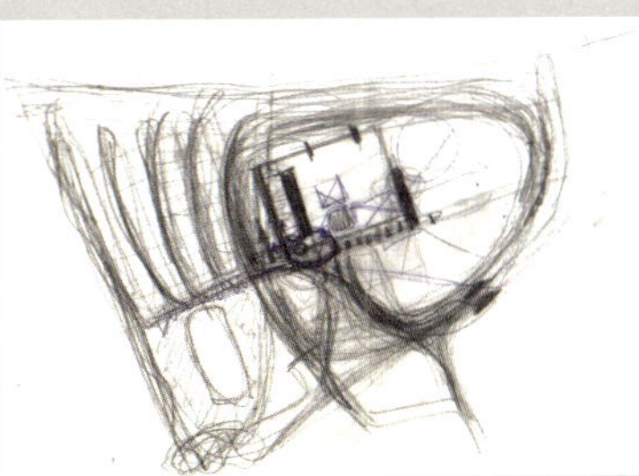

Exhibition
Common ground. 13. Mostra Internazionale di
Architettura, Venice (IT) 2012
with Robbrecht en Daem architecten,
Christina Iglesias, Maarten Vandenabeele

MMXII – 06

Housing with 34 apartments, Academie
Ghent
2012-2022
with Robbrecht en Daem architecten,
Dierendonck Blancke architecten,
architecten Els Claessens en Tania Vandenbussche,
VK Engineering
with the assistance of Bert Callens, Jérôme
Cockerols, Sam De Vocht, Sofie Reynaert,
Marthe Vandenabeele

MMXII – 12

Reconversion House Decaluwé –
Depaepe
Ghent
2012-2014
with the assistance of Peter Vanooteghem

© David Grandorge

MMXIII – 06
Reconversion shop Oorcussen
Ghent
2012-2014
with the assistance of Peter Vanooteghem

MMXIII – 04
House Vandamme – Van Den Abeele
Ghent
2013 – ongoing
with BAS Dirk Jaspaert
with the assistance of Viktor Derks, Sam De Vocht

Exhibition
Abe Bonnema Award. Fries Museum,
Leeuwaarden (NL) 2013

Furniture

tuin-straat-lamp
Ghent
2013, 2021
with Atelier Fé, Jeroen Heerwegh
with the assistance of Sylvie Cosyns,
Sam De Vocht

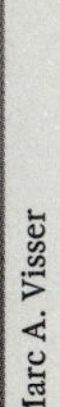
© Marc A. Visser

MMXIII – 08

Verapaz Bridge and inner city ring road
Ghent
2013-2025
competition design, laureate
with Maat ontwerpers, Witteveen + Bos
with the assistance of Jan Baes, Sylvie Cosyns,
Jessica Langerock, Carmen Osten

MMXIV – 01

Reconversion House Huyghe – Libeert
Monte Argentario (IT)
2014-2017
with the assistance of Viktor Derks, Sam De Vocht

MMXIV – 02

Suburban housing with
62 semi-detached homes
Boortmeerbeek
2014-2023
with Bureau Bouwtechniek
with the assistance of Sylvie Cosyns,
Lennert Dejonghe, Viktor Derks, Indra Janda

MMXIV – 03

Reconversion House De Clercq
Hansbeke
2014-2018
with BAS Dirk Jaspaert
with the assistance of Menno Vanderghote

MMXIV – 05

Reconversion House and studio
Phlips – Davans
Ghent
2014-2019
with the assistance of Sylvie Cosyns, Sam De Vocht

MMXIV – 06

Housing for the elderly, Donzapark
Deinze
2014-2021
with Bureau Bouwtechniek, Engitop
with the assistance of Céline De Clercq,
Lennert Dejonghe, Sam De Vocht, Indra Janda,
Menno Vanderghote

Exhibition
Made in Europe. 25 years Mies van der Rohe
Awards, Venice (IT) 2014

Exhibition
Kunstenfestival van de Traagheid, SLOW (36h).
Concert Hall, Bruges (BE) 2014
with a cinematographic portrait by
Maarten Vanden Abeele

MMXV – 03

Reconversion housing and consultation
spaces De Bruecker – Van der Linden –
Versyp
Ghent
2015-2024
with BAS Dirk Jaspaert
with the assistance of Sylvie Cosyns,
Sam De Vocht, Daniel Pickering, Alice Sanders

MMXV – 04

Housing with 99 apartments, Beukenhof
Koksijde
2015-2021
with Pieter Popeye architecten
with the assistance of Sylvie Cosyns, Lennert
Dejonghe, Indra Janda, Marthe Vandenabeele,
Menno Vanderghote

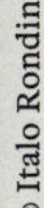
© Italo Rondinella

© Arnout Fonck

MMXV – 06

Pedestrian bridge

Nevele
2015, unbuilt
competition design
with BAS Dirk Jaspaert
with the assistance of Sam De Vocht

MMXV – 14

Portus Ganda

Ghent
2015, unbuilt
competition design
with Robbrecht en Daem architecten, Dierendonck
Blancke architecten, Ney & Partners
with the assistance of Jan Baes, Simon Ceuterick,
Robbrecht Debaillie, Sam De Vocht, Jessica
Langerock, Colm mac Aoidh, Joris Van Huychem

Exhibition
De Wonderjaren. Flanders Architecture
Institute, Cultural Centre Sharpoord, Knokke
(BE) 2015

Exhibition
mOmenten. Parcours in the city centre, Ghent
(BE) 2015

MMXV – 17

Masterplan and reconversion of a historic town centre

Torhout
2015, unbuilt
competition design
with José Maria Sanchez architects,
Maat Ontwerpers, BAS Dirk Jaspaert, Snoeck &
Partners
with the assistance of Viktor Derks, Sam De Vocht,
Javier Fernandez Contreras, Eduardo Mediero,
Daniel Pickering

© Stijn Bollaert

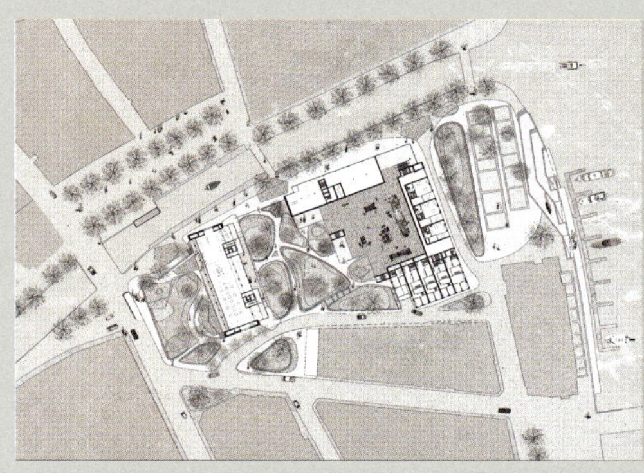

MMXV – 08
Reconversion House De Wilde
Ghent
2015-2019
with BAS Dirk Jaspaert
with the assistance of Sam De Vocht,
Marthe Vandenabeele

MMXV – 09
Reconversion House Van Tornhout
Nevele
2015 – ongoing
with BAS Dirk Jaspaert
with the assistance of Jessica Langerock

MMXV – 11
House Van Hee – Coppens
Bachte-Maria-Leerne, Deinze
2015, unbuilt
with the assistance of Menno Vanderghote

MMXV – 12
Housing with 4 single family homes
Bachte-Maria-Leerne, Deinze
2015-2024
with BAS Dirk Jaspaert
with the assistance of Sylvie Cosyns, Viktor Derks,
Marthe Vandenabeele, Menno Vanderghote

MMXVI – 06
Urban study for housing and recreation, Plaza
Knokke
2016 – ongoing
with Robbrecht en Daem
with the assistance of Bert Callens, Robrecht
Debaillie, Suzanne Desmet, Florence Himpe,
Trice Hofkens, Jérôme Kockerols,
Marthe Vandenabeele

MMXVI – 08
House and apartment Palm – Bossaert
Ghent
2016-2021
with BAS Dirk Jaspaert
with the assistance of Céline De Clercq,
Sam De Vocht

© Viktor Derks

© Viktor Derks

MMXVI – 12

Housing with 87 semi-detached houses and 24 apartments for the elderly

Boutersem
2016 – unbuilt
with the assistance of Jan Baes, Céline De Clercq,
Lennert Dejonghe, Viktor Derks, Daniel Pickering

<u>Exhibition</u>
20 January, in 8.44 / out 8.16. Princeton
University School of Architecture, New Jersey
(USA) 2017
Organised by Drawing Matter (UK)

© Drawing Matter

MMXVII – 06
House Van Hee – Wynant
Bachte-Maria-Leerne, Deinze
2017-2023
with BAS Dirk Jaspaert
with the assistance of Lennert Dejonghe,
Menno Vanderghote

MMXVII – 07
Offices De Witte
Lokeren
2017-2023
with BAS Dirk Jaspaert
with the assistance of Sam De Vocht, Jessica
Langerock

<u>Furniture</u>

dien-blad-koffer
Ghent
2017
with Frank Ternier
by request of Amaryllis Jacobs, Maniera
Brussels
with the assistance of Lennert Dejonghe

© Filip Dujardin

MMXVII – 09
House Vermeiren

Ghent
2017 – ongoing
with BAS Dirk Jaspaert
with the assistance of Céline De Clercq,
Alice Sanders

<u>Exhibition</u>
Maniera 16. Maniera Brussels (BE) 2017
with Marie Mees and Cathérine Biasino
Organised by Amaryllis Jacobs

© Filip Dujardin

© Kristien Daem

MMXVIII – 03

House Dewaegheneire – Walworth

Sint-Niklaas
2018–2022
with Pascal De Munck
with the assistance of Viktor Derks

MMXVIII – 06

Restaurant and hotel Dhooghe – Sulmon

Lede
2018 – unbuilt
with BAS Dirk Jaspaert
with the assistance of Viktor Derks,
Lennert Dejonghe

<u>Exhibition</u>
Freespace. 16. Mostra Internazionale di
Architettura, Venice (IT) 2018
with Kris Martin and Dirk Braeckman

© Stefano Graziani

Daniel Rosbottom @DanielRosbottom · 27 mei
A glowing Marie-Jose van Hee stands in the #Freespace of her exquisitely
simple #venicearchitecturebiennale2018 installation: two lecterns, two books,
two benches, two pictures and two lights - one natural.

<u>Exhibition</u>
Opening Lines. Tchoban Foundation Museum
of Architectural Drawing, Berlin (DE) 2018
Organised by Drawing Matter (UK)

MMXIX – 01

House Verheye – Demol

Duffel
2019-2023
with BAS Dirk Jaspaert
with the assistance of Wannes De Brouwer,
Viktor Derks

MMXIX – 03

House Dubois

Ghent
2019 – ongoing
with Pascal De Munck
with the assistance of Sylvie Cosyns

MMXIX – 04

Housing Portus Ganda

Ghent
2019 – ongoing
with BM engineering, Daidalos Peutz
with the assistance of Wannes De Brouwer, Viktor
Derks, Thomas Faes, Marthe Vandenabeele

MMXIX – 06

House Vandoorne Feys – Greeve

Bornem
2019-2024
with BAS Dirk Jaspaert
with the assistance of Wannes De Brouwer,
Céline De Clercq, Lennert Dejonghe, Thomas Faes,
Uršula Novak, Alice Sanders

Exhibition
*Alternative Historie*s. 6 Cork Street, London
(UK) and CIVA Brussels (BE) 2019
Organised by Drawing Matter and the
Architecture Foundation (UK)

MMXIX – 09

Porter's Lodge Van Hee

Ghent
2019-2024
with Pascal De Munck
with the assistance of Viktor Derks

MMXIX – 10

House Castelein – De Vos

Oostduinkerke
2019-2024
with studiebureau Tecclem
with the assistance of Sylvie Cosyns, Thomas Faes,
Menno Vanderghote

© Sylvie Cosyns

MMXX – 01

House, bakery and chambres d'hôtes
Gutt – Deslypere

Jandrenouille
2020 – ongoing
with BAS Dirk Jaspaert
with the assistance of Wannes De Brouwer,
Sam De Vocht, Frédéric Timmermans

MMXX – 08

Warehouse, offices and production site for a biodynamic winery

Le Puy-Notre-Dame, Maine-et-Loire (FR)
2020 – unbuilt
with BAS Dirk Jaspaert
with the assistance of Wannes De Brouwer,
Sam De Vocht, Thomas Faes, Alice Sanders,
Frédéric Timmermans

MMXXI – 10

House Vindevogel

Oudenaarde
2021 – ongoing
with the assistance of Thomas Faes

MMXXI – 13

Studiolos estate Reuversweerd

Brummen (NL)
2021 – ongoing
with the assistance of Wannes De Brouwer,
Viktor Derks, Sam De Vocht, Thomas Faes

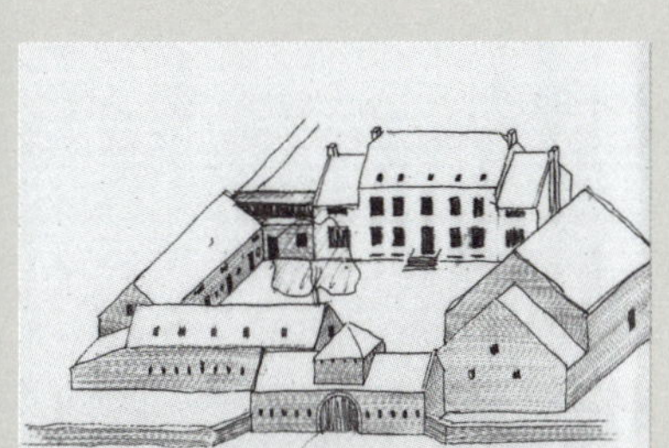

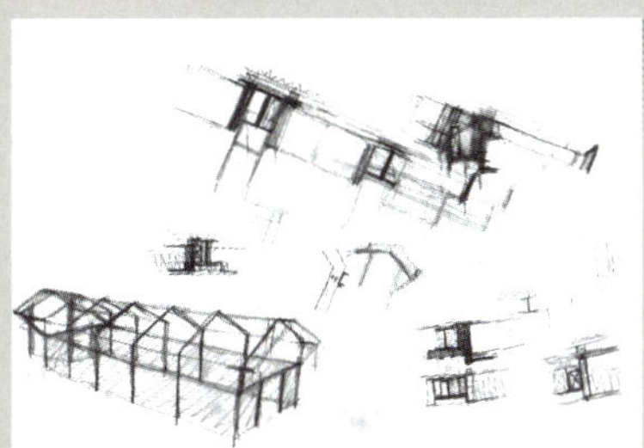

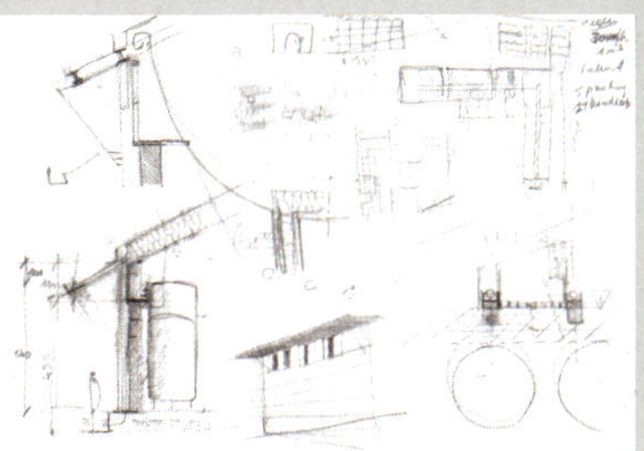

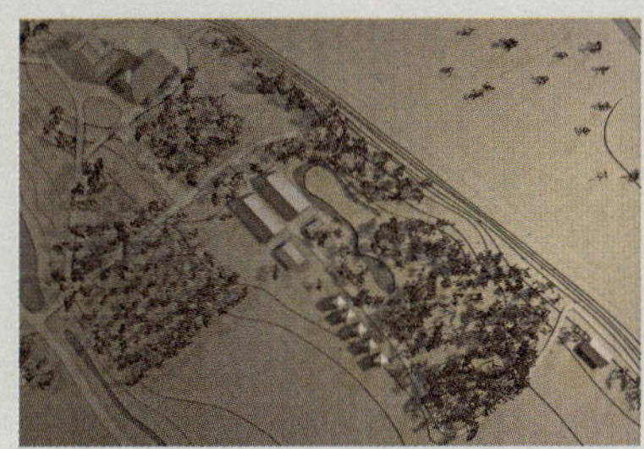

Exhibition
Marie-José Van Hee architecten. A Walk.
De Singel, Antwerp (BE) 2022
Organised by the Flanders Architecture
Institute

Exhibition
Marie-José Van Hee architecten. A Walk.
De Singel, Antwerp (BE) 2022
Organised by the Flanders Architecture
Institute

© Michiel De Cleene

Award
Marie-José Van Hee
Ultima, Flanders Architecture Award,
Brussels (BE) 2023

Award
Marie-José Van Hee
15th Alvar Aalto Medal, Jyväskylä (FI) 2024
Awarded by the Alvar Aalto Foundation,
the Architecture and Design Museum Helsinki,
the Finnish Society of Architecture,
the Association of Finnish Architects and the
City of Helsinki.

Exhibition
Marie-José Van Hee. For Sun and Wind to Paint on. Organised by the Architecture and Design Museum Helsinki (FI) 2025. Traveling to the Alvar Aalto Museum Jyväskylä (FI) 2025

© Maija Holma

frontcover: House HdF, Zuidzande, 2007-2011
backcover: House Van Hee, Ghent, 1994-1997